CW00797006

The
Three Faces of Monotheism

OTHER BOOKS BY GEORGE FRANKL

The End of War or the End of Mankind (1955)

I find myself very much in agreement with your point of view.

Bertrand Russell (*Letter to the author, 22. VI. 55*)

The Failure of the Sexual Revolution (1974)

The sexual revolution has at last found its historian in George Frankl. He has something illuminating to say on almost every aspect of the subject.

E. Hutber, *Sunday Telegraph*

The Social History of the Unconscious (1989)

...incomparable erudition. His knowledge in areas so diverse as history, archaeology, languages, arts and literature, sociology, etc., is absolutely impressive.

Alexander Dimitrijevic,
Faculty of Philosophy, Department of Psychology, Belgrade.

The Unknown Self (1990)

... profound insights, humanity and passion.

Stephen Davy, *Oxford Times*

Exploring the Unconscious (1994)

Anyone wishing to understand what psychoanalysts are talking about must read this book ... If it stimulates more people to use Frankl's ideas and methods so much to the good: the world needs more competent and dedicated therapists.

Sylvia Justice-Mills, *Psychodynamic Counselling*

Foundations of Morality (2000)

Can psychoanalysis, addressing human nature generally, help establish a universal ground for morality? ... George Frankl admirably has undertaken a broad exploration and synthesis of such questions ...

Samuel T. Goldberg,
Journal of the American Psychoanalytic Association

Blueprint for a Sane Society (2004)

... in the great tradition of humanistic writings ... We need a George Frankl.

Prof. Nicholas Williams, Saitama Institute of Technology

The Three Faces of Monotheism

JUDAISM CHRISTIANITY ISLAM

GEORGE FRANKL

OPEN GATE PRESS

incorporating Centaur Press

LONDON

First published in 2005 by Open Gate Press
51 Achilles Road, London NW6 1DZ

British Library Cataloguing-in-Publication Programme
A catalogue record for this book is available from the British Library.

ISBN 1 871871 63 8

Printed and bound in Great Britain by Bell & Bain Ltd., Glasgow.

CONTENTS

Prologue

I began to write the first two sections of this book, Judaism and Christianity, nearly twenty years ago and did not attempt to publish it. On thinking back now, I realise that I was stimulated to investigate the rise of the two great monotheistic religions by the many discussions I had with my good friend Hyam Maccoby who was deeply immersed in Judaism and committed to its ideas, devoting himself to the study of its history and theological concepts. Above all he was determined to clarify who Jesus was, both as a person and how he came to be the founder of Christianity. Like many other researchers, he determined to find out how the young Jewish rabbi came to be presented in the New Testament not only as the founder of Christianity but also as the Son of God, crucified to atone for the sins of mankind and worshipped as God. Like many Jews, he could not believe in this story, nor that a Jewish preacher could present himself as God's only beloved Son or being like God, and that he was sacrificed by God to save humanity from its state of sinfulness, and indeed, from its fall from Grace. He subjected the Gospel story to a meticulous investigation of the Roman occupation and the role of Pontius Pilate in the murder of Yeshua.

As a Jew he was of course particularly outraged by the claim of Christianity that it was the Jews who were responsible for the murder of Christ. This accusation has branded them as God-killers in the mind of Christendom, and imposed a heavy burden of guilt upon the Jews, and they had to suffer the hatred and ruthless persecution to which they were subjected for nearly two thousand years. Of course I knew about anti-Semitism but listening to Hyam's story of the deliberate misrepresentation of historical truth, the ruthless manipulation of facts which has turned much of Christianity into a pack of lies presented as dogma, and the vicious dogma of mankind's sinfulness, only to be redeemed by the worship of Jesus who had to suffer the torments of the Cross for the sins of humanity, impelled me to study this dismal history in detail and provide a psychoanalytic explanation for this religious pathology which has overtaken the mind of Christianity. Just as I have encouraged Hyam to write a full exposé of his findings, I encouraged myself to write down what I had found out in my own researches.

But I hesitated to publish it as my mind turned to an analysis of mankind's evolution which could explain the origins of cultures, religions and the need for a God in the first place. I wanted to apply my discoveries of the unconscious mind of individuals to the collective memories and their evolution through history from the very beginning to our own time. I did this in my other books, and had almost forgotten the work I had done on Judaism and Christianity – until September 11th and the shock of a barbarism that erupted into the Western world after some seven hundred years since the coming of the Middle Ages.

It became clear to me that the three monotheistic religions are interrelated by their claim to be descended from the God of Abraham, and that the reasons for their turning from the ideal of the divine father uniting mankind in his fatherhood and degenerating into hatred for each other demanded explanation.

George Frankl,
December 2004

PART 1   Judaism

Judaism

THE EMERGENCE OF MONOTHEISM

Ten thousand years ago many patriarchal cultures emerged in the Middle East, from Jericho and Çatal Hüyük to Assyria, Egypt and Babylon. However, about 1800 BC the first idea of a truly universal God, the Creator of the universe and of humanity, arose and communicated his purpose and his aims for mankind in the religion of Judaism, initiated by Abraham, codified by Moses and proclaimed by the prophets. Monotheism was a decisive step forward in religious as well as political thought. The Greek idealization of the human being, largely freed from the need to identify with a deity, made philosophy as we know it possible. Judaic monotheism and Greek philosophy represent the consolidation and high culture of patriarchy, and Western civilisation has inherited their aspirations as well as their conflicts.

1. THE ONE AND ONLY GOD

The Athenians replaced the gods by the affirmation of reason. In the tradition of the Greek philosophers we restitute God in ourselves; through the affirmation of reason he is reborn in our soul.

The Jews conceived another form by which the male of patriarchy came to be presented. Having overcome the gods of

3

Mesopotamia and Egypt and, in particular, freed themselves from the domain of the goddesses of matriarchal cultures whose spouses, sons and consorts the male gods of those civilisations were meant to be, they proclaimed the ultimate supremacy of the mature male and his omnipotence by his idealised projection upon the One God who alone made the world and who reigns supreme over everything he created. He has eliminated all the goddesses and all their spouses from the heavens; he is the sole creator, the *causa prima*, the agent of life, the embodiment of purpose and reason, of fate and eternity. His will and his purpose give meaning to all that exists, and the lives of men reflect his intentions; through his purpose men's history emerges as a movement towards the goal that God has set before them; through him men expected to acquire great powers, the knowledge of the essence and purpose of life; through him they hoped to be the masters of fate, the initiators of justice and the creators of laws.

Who were these people who produced the monotheistic revolution that came to be the model and guide that rivalled the humanistic vision of the Greeks, and even more profoundly influenced the development of Western civilisation? Here we confront a difficulty more complex and baffling than found among the Mesopotamian empires, the Egyptians and the Greeks. Indeed, every attempt at historical reconstruction encounters a problem inherent in all historical sciences, but here even more so, for here myth and actuality are so closely interwoven that it is difficult to separate them. Every history has an aspect of myth – a people's idealised self-image that at least colours the events they relate about themselves. But the Jews' image of themselves has been so fundamentally interwoven with the image of their God that they see themselves almost entirely as his children, and their history is really a reflection of God's view of them. It is how God sees them, his experience of them

4

that is revealed in their great writings, their relationship to him, their shortcomings, agonies, trials and triumphs before his gaze. It is really God's experience of his children that is related in their historical chronicle. It is a spiritual history enacted not in some ethereal sphere but on the hard ground of reality.

The chief and almost only source of Jewish history is the Bible. There was, however, a lively literature amongst the Jews at least from the time of David's monarchy at about 1000 BC, but all of these writings are lost and the only evidence of them are their titles which are mentioned tantalisingly in the Bible from time to time. Very recently fascinating confirmation has been found of the antiquity and authenticity of the literary sources behind the Bible.[1] But nevertheless, the first cohesive narration of the Israelites made its first appearance about 850 BC. There are five main texts from which the mythological and historic writings of the Bible were constructed.

> 1. The so-called Yahwist (J) text, representing the mythology of the southern kingdom, Judah, in the ninth century BC. Here the Creator is Yahweh (always translated 'The Lord') and the mountain of the Law is Sinai.
> 2. The so-called Elohim (E) text, representing the mythology of the northern kingdom, Israel, in the eighth century BC. Here the mountain of the Law is Horeb and the Creator is Elohim (intensive plural of the word El, always translated 'God').
> 3. A ritual code known as the 'Code of Holiness' (H), purporting to have been received by Moses on Sinai, but dating apparently from the seventh century BC. Preserved in *Leviticus* xvii-xxvi.
> 4. The text of the Deuteronomists (D). The nucleus of D was almost certainly the 'Scroll of the Law' of 621 BC.
> 5. The post-exilic compound of priestly writings known as the Priestly (P) text, which was proclaimed by the priest Ezra in Jerusalem about 397 BC, amplified and reworked until about 300 BC.

The events to which these writings refer belong to much earlier times, in the same way as Homer's poems written about 800 BC refer to events that took place about 1100 BC. The Israelite literature from the early Yahwist and Elohim texts is chiefly concerned with the times and the person of Abraham who lived about 1900 to 1800 BC, and with Moses and the Exodus about 1400 to 1300 BC. It is likely that these texts incorporate written material dating from the time of Moses, or even composed by Moses himself. Many of these writings were regarded with great reverence and were preserved as 'memorials and testimonials'. "And the Lord said unto Moses: 'Write this for a memorial in a book and report it in the ears of Joshua'" (*Exodus* xvii, 14). But all these texts and memorials were not yet collected into a single authoritative book.

This happened with the 'Deuteronomic movement' during the reign of King Josiah of Judah (640-609 BC). It is interesting to note that many scholars think it is likely that the book was composed somewhat earlier, in the reign of Josiah's grandfather Manasseh, who was a renegade against the God of Israel, and even converted the temple in Jerusalem into a place of idolatrous worship. Manasseh's father had been the pious King Hezekiah, whose reign had assumed messianic stature when the kingdom of Judah was miraculously saved from the onslaught of the Assyrians. In the shock and guilt of Manasseh's apostasy, the Book of Deuteronomy was composed as a rallying-point for the faithful, and became the nucleus of the Bible.

The older writings containing stories of the patriarchs, of the Exodus from Egypt, the Revelation on Sinai, and the corpora of laws, were gathered by members of the Deuteronomic movement and rewritten and edited into a five-volume book which became the Torah (literally: teaching). The Deuteronomic movement also undertook the editing and composition of books of history, telling the story of the people of Israel from the time

6

of entry into the Promised Land down to their own day. These texts received their final revision and co-ordination with the additions of the writings of the prophets in the Priestly text composed between 397 BC and 300 BC. Thus it took nearly seven hundred years before the Bible took its final shape and assumed the position of centrality in thought and worship that it has had since.

However, while the Deuteronomic movement and the later Priestly edition dealt with events far back in history, they would be interpreted and coloured by the religious imagination and concepts of their Deuteronomic and Priestly writers. The ideas which prevailed between 600 and 300 BC would be retro-projected into the past; the stories dealing with those early times, the ancestral figure of Abraham and the laws received by Moses, would be mythologised to reflect the images and beliefs which prevailed during the time of their writers and editors.

The Jewish concept of God represents a remarkably high level of abstract thought. While the Hebrews invented the idea of monotheism, their God does not appear in terms of an anthropomorphic image. He is not presented in a perceptual, bodily form, but as a cosmic spirit, endowed with will, purpose and intelligence, and revealed to man by His words and His commandments. His eternity and omnipotence transcend the limitations of time and space to which human perception and understanding are bound. In Kantian terms we could say he is unaffected by the human categories of perception and the understanding, i.e. time, space, substance and causality. He is the cause of all things, but he is not caused by anything and thus not subject to causality. He is the beginning of time but not limited to time because he is eternal. He exists but he is not perceptible, and unlike Zeus he is not subject to any other power such as fate, for he is fate. He is both existence and essence, he is the One and the many, for all that exists is his emanation.

The world of existence is a manifestation of his will and his thought. He is not a phenomenon but a noumenon, and all phenomena, all existing and perceptible things, including man, are the expression, the embodiment of his mind. But he reveals himself to his highest and latest creation mankind by the laws inscribed on the tablets of stone and by the words which he speaks to the prophets. Indeed, the history of mankind reveals His purpose, and the holy script, the Bible, shows man's struggle towards fulfilment of the purpose he has in mind for them; and it shows the divine mission of the Jewish people to be an example to mankind, and their failures, their agonies and their successes.

Being timeless, this God has no history; he is not born, he has no parents, he has no love affairs, does not get married, nor does he die. But his creations, and in particular his most interesting and rather special creation, mankind, have a history. He gave birth to mankind and assigned to it a purpose, and in pursuit of this purpose it acquires a history. He implanted a soul and a rational faculty in men to enable them to comprehend the meaning of the words which he spoke, but he has also given them freedom, a capacity for choice by which they can transcend their natural limitations and reach out towards an understanding of his vision. He gave them the ability to grow, to learn, and to perfect themselves, the freedom to choose between wisdom or ignorance, good or evil, and to fulfil his purpose by their efforts.

Why, it can be asked, and it is often asked in desperation, has God not given mankind perfection in order to accomplish his aims? Why has he given them the freedom to be evil and ignorant when he could easily have made them wise and good? The answer must be that men could not have comprehended a God who ignores their manifold destructive, aggressive, narcissistic, egocentric, greedy and selfish impulses. As men are

8

only too aware of their destructive and anti-social drives as well as their desire for love and friendship, they need a God who understands their conflicts; who, furthermore, responds to them emotionally with love or anger, for otherwise he would appear distant and indifferent and his expectations would become a burden rather than guide. The sons need their father's human proximity, his emotional involvement, in order to feel accepted and assured of his love. But nevertheless, being a father his love is not unconditional: he expects his sons to improve themselves and to learn, for otherwise there would be no progress, no growth, and men would remain bound to their limitations. He is teacher as well as supporter. It is his duty to ensure that his sons acquire knowledge and skills, and he has to threaten and punish them sometimes as well as showing his love.

This rather strange seeming combination between a formless essence and a paternal figure in the Jewish concept of 'the God' represents men's deep experience of their superego. On the one hand, it is an emanation of the unconscious sensation of the father's presence as an unformed energy, whose power and whose will is sensed and his voice heard by the child during its pre-ego, pre-verbal stages of development, and the later experience of him as an all-powerful being whose expectations and demands lie on the man's mind as a source of hope or fear.

While it is a fundamental premise of Jewish theology that God only appears to man through the words of his prophets and the laws inscribed on the tablets of stone and the holy scriptures, the Jewish vision of God appears from the earliest moments of the Bible. The eternal essence that creates all life and builds universes directs his attention to the making of the earth:

In the beginning God created the heavens and the earth. The earth was without form and void, and the darkness was upon the face of the deep; and the Spirit of God was moving over the face of the waters...

Genesis i, 1-2.

And after he made the earth and the heavens and created all forms of life upon it, he said:

> 'Let us make man in our image, and after our likeness...' So God created man in his own image, in the image of God he created him; male and female he created them... And God said to them, 'Be fruitful and multiply, and fill the earth and subdue it; and have dominion over the fish of the sea and over the birds of the air and over every living thing that moves upon the earth.'

Genesis i, 26-28.

Theologians and philosophers through the ages have attempted to clarify the meaning of the statement that God created man in his own image. Was God then a man who reproduced the human being in his likeness as a mirror image of himself? This contradicts the notion of God as a universal and immortal being, for man is mortal and limited and certainly has not been given the quality of omnipotence. It must be the expectations which the father has of the boy and the boy's need to see him as a model for himself that the statement that God made man in his image can be understood. God did not make man in the image which he has of himself but in the image which he has of man, what God wants man to be and what he expects of him. For it is an important factor in a person's development that he acquires an internal awareness of the father's image of him, and his self-image will largely depend upon how father sees him, or how a man believes his father sees him and what he wants him to be.

The error of considering that God has created man as a replica of himself has also evoked puzzlement about the statement that he not only made man the male, but man and woman

10

in his own image. For how could a male God have created a woman in his image? This had led the Cabbalists to conclude that God must be an hermaphrodite, combining the male and female characteristics in his own person. This certainly is a great advance over the traditional concept of the male tyrant who sees everything through masculine eyes, as it grants full equality to the sexes in the eyes of God, a sense of unity between them as human beings.

It is true to say that God, being primarily male, is also a protective parent-figure, combining in himself the mother's protective qualities with the father's strength and power; and the earliest impressions of the mother continue to be found in him; although on the level of the growing boy he is the paternal superego, for the girl he becomes the object of adoration and dependency. It is this dual role which is emphasised in man's consciousness of the patriarchal God.

Now after he had created man and woman, he placed them in the secure and plentiful world of the Garden of Eden. The Garden of Eden no doubt symbolises every man's fantasy of infancy and childhood, enveloped by love and security without conditions. But He put his tree into the middle of this natural cradle, this primeval home of man, to make his presence and his power felt. He is the one in possession of knowledge (and knowledge here also means sexual knowledge, which is His privilege). The tree represents his male power and penis, which the children must not approach. It is the energy which brings forth life and fertility, and the children must be protected from the sexual sensations which emanate from it, and, in turn, it must be protected from the girl's desire and the boy's feeling of envy. For if the children were to approach it and partake of its fruits, they would experience the power of sexual sensations, become excited and lose their innocence.

Patriarchal children subjected to maturation delay and sexual repression must be prevented from acquiring sexual maturity too early lest it disrupt the innocence of childhood and respect for the father's authority. For it is the father's authority, and his exclusive rights to sexuality, that keeps the family together. The boy in particular must be protected from too early an acquisition of sexual desire and knowledge, for it would make him feel prematurely grown-up and rebellious.

However, sooner or later the pubertal drives make themselves felt, and sexual longings and sexual curiosity break through the taboos. The father's sexuality arouses the curiosity of the daughter and the envy of the son. Eve, at first still the child-woman, cannot resist the temptations of the snake, the undulating sexual sensations that the phallus arouses in her. The snake is both phallus as well as the girl's own erotic sensations, and she sees the father's sexual representation – the snake – in the Garden, and her erotic impulses impel her to reach out to it and take from its fruit. And she hands the fruit to Adam so that he can experience its power. And as soon as Adam tastes the fruit and eats it, he is filled with sexual knowledge and they are no longer innocent children. Her desire is for Adam, and he wants to take the father's place. But the father becomes anxious that the boy Adam will want to be like God, that he will want to replace Him:

> Behold, the man has become like one of us, knowing good and evil; and now, lest he put forth his hand and take also of the tree of life, and eat, and live forever – therefore the Lord God sent him forth from the Garden of Eden.
>
> *Genesis* iii, 22-23.

The tree of life is the life of God, the God of life. And the father feels he will be usurped and eliminated from his position of supremacy, and possibly, his life itself threatened by the man

Adam. And Adam and Eve have to leave this home, now that they are no longer children, and have to go out into the world, and by their own efforts and labours and skills build their own home, eventually to transform the world outside into a home fit for grown-ups, and in the fullness of their maturity transform the whole earth into a Garden of Eden. And that is the goal which God sets before them to be fulfilled in the Messianic age. And God does not forsake them after their expulsion from Eden; he will give them laws and he will speak to them, and he implants a soul capable of receiving knowledge into them, so that they can comprehend and follow his instructions. When the time is ripe a prophet – Moses – will arise who will receive God's instruction and hand it over to man, and other prophets and teachers will follow to continue the instruction of men and remind them of God's thought and guide them on to the right path.

But it is not long before God has to face the complexities and contradictions of the human condition. The very first children of Eve, Cain and Abel, were unable to live in peace with each other:

> Now Abel was a keeper of sheep, and Cain a tiller of the ground. In the course of time Cain brought to the Lord an offering of the fruit of the ground, and Abel brought of the firstlings of his flock and of their fat portions. And the Lord had regard for Abel and his offering, but for Cain and his offering he had no regard. So Cain was very angry, and his countenance fell. The Lord said to Cain, 'Why are you so angry, and why has your countenance fallen? If you do well, will you not be accepted? And if you do not well, sin is couching at the door; its desire is for you, but you must master it.'
>
> *Genesis* iv, 2-7.

There have been innumerable attempts to analyse the meaning

of these cryptic passages in terms of the custom of human sacrifice. In particular the last lines have evoked puzzlement and
argument. However, the first question which springs to mind is:
Why has God rejected the sacrificial gift of the agriculturalist,
yet responded with satisfaction to the gifts of the herdsman?
Could it merely be that he preferred meat to vegetables? Could
this simple preference on the part of God be held responsible
for creating that rivalry that produced the primeval horror of
brother-murder? And why was God so callous as to let his tastes
and preference bring about a sense of grievous rejection in one
of his sons? After all, he had commanded men to till the ground
and eat the plants of the field, and Cain, the farmer, had obeyed
God's instruction. Here we may find the clue to the problem.
Tilling the ground and eating of bread is the fate of men expelled
from paradise, whereas in Eden they had eaten the meat of
sheep and cattle. The rule of having to labour on the ground
for sustenance that applied to men in their exile could not have
applied to God, and He would consider Cain's offering as a
presumption in comparing himself to God, of forgetting God's
privileges and so reducing Him to his own status. God is prepared to forgive him if Cain would offer him the best meat
from sheep, indeed he tells him that it is right for him to kill
sheep and cattle for this purpose. But should he refuse to do
this, then sin is 'couching at the door'; the sin he commits will
threaten to overwhelm him, take possession of him and lead
him to self-destruction.

The sin here lies in Cain's presumption of putting himself
on the same level as God, and assuming that what is good
enough for Cain must be good enough for God. This presumption made him forget his subservience to God. Cain did
not understand God's warning and instruction, or did not wish
to submit to it. Perhaps the pleasure of his sin had already
entered into his soul, and he revenged himself upon the favoured

14

brother and killed him. Added to this is the fact that Cain was the first-born, and as such the one who poses the main threat to the father; for in his childhood he had sole affection of mother and would be most reluctant to relinquish her. The meat he should have offered God in sacrifice also symbolises, on the genital level, the flesh – the mother – meant for God's delectation as his right. The animals of the earth are symbolic representations of the mother; in their sacrifice the male sacrifices his sexual desire for the mother and relinquishes her to the father as a recognition of his primacy, his *jus primae noctis*. But Cain did not do this and therefore he could no longer till the earth which is the father's possession, and he was cast out once more to be a wanderer.

It is important to realise that with the patriarchal revolution, consolidated and brought to its fullest expression by the Jews, the nature of sacrifice underwent a fundamental change. As we have seen, sacrifice is above all a gift-offering to God; its emphasis is upon a gift rather than the killing. The killing is only a sign of willingness, of submission to the demands of God. Instead of eating the sacrificial animal, one first gives it to the divinity. In matriarchal cultures the most attractive young man of the tribe is offered to the goddess as a consort for her gratification and he was rarely killed. When, however, she had become angry at the male's refusal to satisfy her and her desire was dominated by sadistic drives, he had to be killed, and it was the blood from his body that becomes her elixir, his libido which she absorbed for her delectation.

Oral-sadistic drives and the cannibalistic *vagina dentata* assumed primacy over the oral and genital primacies of love. Thus human sacrifice, the killing of the young male, was primarily a late matriarchal ritual.

In Judaic monotheism such a sacrifice is an abomination to the God who sees in the man an emanation of Himself, his

15

product and his companion. Therefore, the killing of Abel is an abomination in Yahweh's eyes. And still he does not kill Cain but once more expels him from the land, as he had expelled Adam from paradise. And He is even prepared to protect him in his journeyings through strange lands. Cain is given a sign that although he has been expelled, God still protects him and does not allow anyone to kill him. The earth belongs to Him, he has created her from his Spirit and by his labours; (as Adam produced the woman out of his rib, his phallus, as Aphrodite arose out of Kronos' genitals, and Athene was born from Zeus' head) she is Yahweh's consort and He fructified her and made her bring forth life, and humans are his favourite children for he has equipped them with a measure of understanding, an ability to hear his words and to respond to them. He has given them some aspects of himself, and wants them to husband the earth, to till it and make it fruitful:

> And the desolate land shall be tilled, whereas it lay desolate in the sight of all that passed by. And they shall say, 'This land that was desolate is become like the Garden of Eden... '
>
> *Ezekiel* xxxvi, 34-35.

Neither God nor the Earth want men to be sacrificed. Whereas in the past the angry mother-goddess demanded the blood of men, she now repudiates this offering. It is no longer necessary, so that when Cain murdered Abel, the Lord said:

> 'What have you done? The voice of your brother's blood is crying to me from the ground. And now you are cursed from the ground, which has opened its mouth to receive your brother's blood from your hand. When you till the ground, it shall no longer yield to you its strength; and you shall be a fugitive and a wanderer on the earth.'
>
> *Genesis* iv, 10-12.

16

The earth opens up to receive the blood of the slain brother; she does accept his soul, but she curses the killer, for there was no need for his blood. She wants man's attention and his love that cleaves to her with his ploughshares and fertilises her. But now that Cain has unnecessarily and sinfully spilled his brother's blood, she repudiates him and will no longer respond to his labours, and he will be a fugitive and a wanderer on the earth.

> And Adam knew his wife again, and she bore a son and called his name Seth, for she said, 'God has appointed for me another child instead of Abel, for Cain slew him.' To Seth also a son was born, and he called his name Enoch. At that time men began to call upon the name of the Lord.
>
> *Genesis* iv, 25-26.

Men multiplied and there was much wickedness among them. The earth was corrupt in God's sight and was filled with violence. And often God became angry and decided to make an end to this race, but again and again he relented. He decided to make a covenant with one particular people and implant his Spirit into their souls to be his Chosen People, an example to mankind.

2. ABRAHAM'S CALL

He chose a man called Abraham, and He said to him:

> 'Go from your country and your kindred and your father's house to the land that I will show you. And I will make of you a great nation, and I will bless you, and make your name great, so that you will be a blessing. I will bless those who bless you, and him who curses you I will curse; and by you all the families of the earth shall bless themselves.'
>
> *Genesis* xii, 1-3.

The Bible reports that Abraham moved with his father and his family from Ur in southern Mesopotamia to Haran in the north and they settled there. It was about 1900 BC. Now it has been seriously questioned by archaeologists and scholars whether Abraham and his ancestors were ever citizens of Ur, the capital of Sumeria. They have cast doubt upon the claims of Sir Leonard Woolley that he uncovered Abraham's town when in 1926 he made his great archaeological discovery which revealed to the world the remains of Ur. At the time of Abraham, and indeed for a long time before, Ur was a prosperous and civilised town with large temples and elegant two-storeyed villas, often containing thirteen rooms and walls neatly covered in plaster and whitewashed.

Wandering through the alleyways of Ur, past the walls of the great temple fringed by trees, Sir Leonard Woolley exclaimed: 'We must radically alter our view of the Hebrew patriarch when we see that his early years were passed in such sophisticated surroundings. He was the citizen of a great city and inherited the traditions of an old and highly organised civilisation.'

This idea was in complete contradiction to the long held view that Abraham was a nomad, or semi-nomad, who brought his nomadic traditions of life to Palestine. According to this view, the early Israelites lived as nomads, and when they came to settle down as a nation they still retained some characteristics of that earlier way of life.

As against this tradition, we have the story of Cain which represents a condemnation of outright nomadism. When he is driven into the desert in punishment for the murder of Abel, he will be a wanderer condemned to lead a nomadic existence, and therefore the desert is presented as an exile for the disgraced settlers, as a punishment, and not as a normal habitation.

While there are many doubts whether Abraham was actually

a citizen of Ur, the evidence available makes it appear fairly certain that Abraham lived in Haran with his father and with his wife Sarah. After all, God did not tell Abraham to leave Ur, but to go out of Haran into Canaan, the land he promised to him.

While until recently nobody knew what place the biblical Haran actually referred to and nothing was known from contemporary references about its early history, scholars had for long been familiar with many Babylonian and Assyrian inscriptions mentioning the royal city of Mari. In 1934 excavations uncovered the remains of this city and it turned out to be one of the great discoveries in the history of archaeology. Archaeologists found a great number of houses and splendid courtyards, over 20,000 clay tablets and a ziggurat with a palace containing some 220 rooms, and in 1938 uncovered the palace of the kings of Mari.

This building, dating to the middle of the third millennium BC, covered almost ten acres. One wing of the palace was used exclusively for religious ceremonies. It also contained a throne room approached by a marvellous staircase. A long, processional way passed through several rooms to the palace chapel. This was the centre both of official life and administration of the kingdom. The entire court lived under the king's roof: ministers, administrators, secretaries and scribes had their own roomy quarters. Archaeologists found almost 24,000 documents. The great find of the tablets at Nineveh was put in the shade by this discovery, since the famous library of the Assyrian king, Ashurbanipal, amounted to a 'mere' 22,000 clay texts. Two tablets contain a list of two thousand craftsmen, giving their full names and the names of their guilds. Numerous orders for the construction of canals, locks, dams and embankments made it plain that the prosperity of the country largely depended on a widespread system of irrigation, which was constantly under the supervision of government engineers, who saw to its care and maintenance.

From the large amount of evidence revealed by these tablets we can form a picture of the organisation and administration of the kingdom of Mari in the nineteenth and eighteenth centuries BC. It is of particular interest to biblical scholars that on many clay tablets discovered at Mari a whole series of familiar sounding names were discovered, names like Peleg and Serug, Nahor and Terah, and – Haran.

Lying in the centre of the Plain of Aram, Haran, according to descriptions, must have been a flourishing city in the nineteenth century BC. The home of Abraham, and thus the birthplace of the Jewish people, is here for the first time historically attested by contemporary texts. We may, therefore, conclude that *even if* Abraham was not a citizen of Ur, he almost certainly had lived with his family in Haran, a provincial capital in the kingdom of Mari, and as such would be a town dweller used to the administrative and commercial institutions of his kingdom and the practices of trade and agriculture. He would not, therefore, have been a nomad but most probably a merchant – and a prosperous one, considering the cost and organisation required to mount an expedition to Canaan some 600 miles distant.

In 1990 BC the first dynasty of Babylon was founded, and under Hammurabi, about 1840 BC, Babylon rose supreme, not only on the riverside zones of Mesopotamia but also on the uplands of Syria and southern Anatolia. The area, which was once the centre of the Halaf culture (indeed, Haran was situated very near the ancient town of Halaf), became a busy centre of commerce, and the use of cuneiform writing, found on the tablets from Mari, brought extensive areas of south-west Asia into fruitful and peaceful contact.

During this period, south-east Anatolia and northern Mesopotamia were marked most significantly by the arrival of Assyrian merchants, and trading-posts were established to operate traffic in raw materials to the south and south-west. Merchandise was carried on the backs of donkeys organised in caravans.

Now it is a matter for conjecture what motivated Abraham to leave Haran and make an expedition to Canaan. It must have been a decision to emigrate and start a new life in another country, using established trade routes to get there. Indeed, he obviously used one of the great trade routes that had led from the Euphrates to Jordan, from the kingdom of Mesopotamia to the Phoenician seaports on the Mediterranean and the distant Nile lands in Egypt. The Bible tells us that Abraham had a vision of God encouraging him to undertake this journey to a land which would become his new home and which He would make into a great and prosperous country for him and his descendants. He might have written his revelations, his hopeful fantasies or visions, on clay tablets, and it could well be that the Israelites were his descendants. They would preserve these tablets as holy script, as a testament of their birthright, and the God who spoke to Abraham would be the eternal and omnipotent protector of this people.

And then these early cuneiform writings, or the oral tradition of them, would be known to later generations of Hebrews, and expanded, elaborated and interpreted according to their theological concepts. It is significant that Abraham did not take his father or his mother or any of his parental relations with him to this new country. Nor are they ever mentioned afterwards. This would have been unusual in those times of strong parental bonds. Neither did Abraham bring his Mesopotamian gods to set them up in this new land. Thus Abraham not only broke away from his parents but also from his culture, rebelling against the gods of his fathers; and it could be that this God who spoke to him was a restitution of the parental gods whom he had denied. And the writing on the tablets, recording His voice, was the sole representation of this new God. Thus the spoken and written word henceforth became the embodiment of the Hebrew God, allowing for no other form.

In the Book of Joshua, God tells the Israelites: 'Long ago your ancestors Terah and his sons Abraham, Nahor and Haran lived beyond the Euphrates and served other gods. Then I took your father Abraham from beyond the River and led him to the land of Canaan.'

But *Genesis* suggests that Abraham's family lived in Ur of the Chaldees in southern Mesopotamia. Archaeologists went looking for Ur, and we are told that *ur* means 'fire' or 'flame' in Hebrew. Suddenly the line, 'I am the Lord who brought you out from the fire of the Chaldeans', took on new meaning.

There is a memorable composition known as 'Lamentation over the destruction of Ur', which gives a graphic description of the devastation wrought by the Elamites, who invaded the city. Part of it reads as follows:

> O father Nanna [the Sumerian moon-god, the god of Ur],
> That city was turned to ruins; the people groan...
>> Its walls were breached; the people groan...
>> Within all its streets, where people used to walk,
>>> corpses lay...
>> Mothers and fathers who did not flee their houses
>>> were destroyed by fire.
>> Babes in arms were carried off by the waters like
>>> fish. [2]
>
> (translated by S. N. Kramer).

It could well be that when as a child or young man Abraham witnessed the fire and devastation of his birthplace it imprinted itself upon his mind as a traumatic experience and prompted him

22

to look for an eternal and all-powerful God who would protect mankind from such catastrophes and guide it towards a secure and peaceful world. Looking for a real meaning in life, he would have rebelled against the pagan religion of his family and his father's idol worship.

Abraham's childhood, which is ignored by the Bible, was recreated by his descendants after his death. Some of their stories were collected in the Book of Jubilees, a non-canonical Jewish text from the second century BC, where the boy Abraham is presented as asking his father, a priest, what advantage idols serve, considering that they are mute. 'I also know that, my son,' Terah replies, 'but what shall I do to the people who have ordered me to serve before them?' In another of these legends Abraham asks his father why he takes idols for gods. At night Abraham looks at the stars and thinks they are gods, until they disappear. The same follows for the moon and sun. Finally he realises that One God must be behind them all. 'I disown your idols,' he says to his father, 'I will turn my face to Him who has created the heavens and the earth. I am no idolater.'

In one of the more famous Jewish legends, Abraham smashes the idols with a stick and attempts to blame the destruction on one of the idols:

> 'Why are you mocking me?' his father asks.
> 'Do these idols know anything? Ask *them* if they are able
>   to speak,' Abraham says.
> 'You know that they cannot speak,' comes the reply. [3]

The stunning similarity of these accounts present two options. One, the stories are true and were actually given by God on Mount Sinai along with the written text in the middle of the second millennium BC. The other option is that the legends of Abraham were composed not by God but by God-intoxicated people. It is interesting to note that these legends developed such currency in the Middle East that Muhammad picked them up from Jewish and Christian traders in Arabia and quoted them in his scriptures. This would corroborate the scholarly view that Islam grew from existing elements in the region, and made them accessible to a new and wider audience.

One unintended lesson of Abraham's childhood is that individuals should feel free to liberate themselves from false religions, even in the face of resistance from their families, their nations or their political leaders. There can be no doubt that Abraham had a vision of the God of the Universe and followed His call 'to go forth from your native land, and from your father's house, into the land I will show you.' When Abraham was old and had prospered in this land, the Lord appeared to him, and said to him:

'I am God Almighty; walk before me, and be blameless. And I will make my covenant between me and you, and will multiply you exceedingly... and you shall be the father of a multitude of nations... I will establish my covenant between me and you and your descendants after you throughout their generations for an everlasting covenant, to be God to you and to your descendants after you. And I will give to you, and to your descendants after you, all the land of Canaan, for an everlasting possession, and I will be their God... This is my covenant, which you shall keep, between me and you and your descendants after you: every male among you shall be circumcised. You shall be circumcised in the flesh of your foreskins, and it shall be a sign of the covenant between me and you.'

Genesis xvii, 1-11.

3. THE COVENANT OF CIRCUMCISION

There is no need to assume, as Freud has done, that this custom or ritual of circumcision was ordained by Moses to make sure that the people whom he led out of Egypt would in no way be inferior to the Egyptians, who had for long adopted this custom in order to show their superiority over other races; and that the later writers of the Bible only inserted this passage and ascribed it to Abraham in order to suppress the Egyptian origins of their religion.[4]

This passage is not some irrelevant insertion into the text but quite obviously was intended to take a position of central importance, meaning to confirm God's covenant with Abraham and His people. The very repetitious wording of it shows God's determination to assure a bond between these people and himself which could not be repudiated henceforth.

The covenant here means that men offered their penis to God and he would have power over it, and it should no longer act in defiance of him or be a source of rebellious estrangement. In turn God would protect his people and never forsake them, because rivalry between gods and sons, and the sense of guilt that had arisen from it, would be abolished forever. The sexual drive would no longer incite the sons against him but, on the contrary, would receive his blessing, and the offspring born of the sexual act would be a glorification of God.

When the Jews engage in sexuality they invoke God's permission and receive his blessing. Thus the sexual act would be a blessing, an affirmation of the covenant. And the children would be offered to God, on the eighth day after the boy's birth, and circumcision would be a sign of God's true paternity, and assurance of his protection. Thus God is the real father of men. In order to bring this home to His people, God announces to Abraham that his wife Sarah, who had until that time remained barren, would conceive of a son at the age of ninety: 'I will bless her and moreover will give you a son by her,' said God to Abraham. And when Sarah laughed at this announcement and was most doubtful whether she could give birth in her old age,

He said: 'Is anything too hard for the Lord?' And the Lord visited Sarah and did to her as he promised, and made her fertile. And she conceived and bore Abraham a son in his old age, and his name was Isaac.

Again it is a story told with many repetitions in order to emphasise that God can enable a woman to have a child even at a very old age when it was thought impossible. Thus the true paternity of God is driven home to be an everlasting reminder to His people.

The covenant was meant to eliminate sexual rivalry and the aggression it evokes between God and man, fathers and sons, to bring about a resolution of the Oedipus complex, and therefore it made human sacrifice unnecessary. For sacrifice fundamentally served to propitiate the angry god or goddess and overcome an unbearable sense of guilt. The only sacrifice which God demanded of men is their acknowledgement of him and to fulfil his purpose. To illustrate this point the Bible relates the story of Isaac's binding, Abraham's readiness to sacrifice his only son to God in obedience to his instruction.

In this story Yahweh introduces a new moral dimension where obedience to God's will is the overriding factor and the readiness for the sacrifice sufficient to make the actual killing unnecessary. It is man's inner acceptance of God's will, his introjection as the God within, as internal presence, which is here being tested and proven:

God said to Abraham, 'Take your son, your only son Isaac, whom you love, and go to the land of Moriah, and offer him there as a burnt offering...' When they came to the place of which God had told him, Abraham built an altar there, and laid the wood in order, and bound Isaac his son, and laid him on the altar, upon the wood. Then Abraham put forth his hand, and took the knife to slay his son. But the angel of the Lord called to him from heaven, and said, 'Abraham, Abraham!'

And he said, 'Here am I.' He said, 'Do not lay your hand on the lad or do anything to him; for now I know that you fear God, seeing you have not withheld your son, your only son, from me.' And Abraham lifted up his eyes and looked, and behold, behind him was a ram, caught in a thicket by his horns; and Abraham went and took the ram, and offered it up as a burnt offering instead of his son. So Abraham called the name of that place, The Lord will provide...

Genesis xxii, 2, 9-14.

On one level we can see in this story a parallel to the Cain and Abel episode and a resolution of the conflict presented there: the killing of a human being is made unnecessary if an animal offered by God is sacrificed to Him. However, it goes much further in the consolidation of God's will in the minds of men. Abraham is both the son of his father – God – as well as the father of his son. He loves his son and at the same time he loves and obeys God, and allows His Spirit to enter into his heart and to dominate and control his ego, to an extent that considerations of self-interest and even love for his son are overridden by the command and laws of God. But once the will of God is accepted by the ego, the conflict between ego and superego is resolved, God's love assured, and the Oedipal sin is redeemed. When God lives within the hearts and minds of men, then external acts of propitiation by means of sacrifice become irrelevant and, indeed, they become a sacrilege, for they show a lapse from the covenant, a sign of estrangement from God. Human sacrifice is also abhorrent to the earth who will mourn the blood spilt on her and curse the killer.

In Abraham's readiness to submit to God's will the first and fundamental step of man's education is completed: he blesses Abraham and he seals the covenant.

'By myself I have sworn, says the Lord, because you have done this, and have not withheld your son, your only son, I will indeed bless you, and I will multiply your descendants as the stars of heaven and as the sand which is on the seashore. And your descendants shall possess the gate of their enemies, and by your descendants shall all the nations of the earth bless themselves, because you have obeyed my voice.'

Genesis xxii, 16-18.

And to this day Jews re-enact the binding of Isaac by binding the tephillin around arm and head to show their readiness to submit to the will of God and to engrave His laws into their minds.

With the internalisation of God into the ego, as the God within, he becomes familiar to the Jews and they enter into a relationship of some intimacy with him. They can speak to God as he can speak to them. When the Lord decided to destroy Sodom and Gomorrah, Abraham stood before him and said to him:

'Wilt Thou indeed destroy the righteous with the wicked?... Far be it from thee to do such a thing, so that the righteous fare as the wicked! Far be that from thee! Shall not the Judge of all the earth do right?'

Genesis xviii, 23, 25.

But it took a long time before the Jews came to establish their nation. The idea that every Jew (i.e. every human being conscious of being the son of God) has a personal relationship with God and does not need to worship any other authority would have made the establishment of nationhood rather problematical. For people who feel themselves in contact with the God of the universe will not easily be prepared to submit to the vagaries of kingship and national authority. Indeed, they would adopt somewhat anarchical attitudes and resent the presumptions of kings and rulers, they would become 'stiff-necked' and querulous towards the authorities that rule nations. Thus, from

28

the very beginning of Jewish history the confrontation between men and God and the covenant between them took precedence over the imperatives of nationhood which dominated all other cultures.

However, God had decided to make the descendants of Abraham into a great nation, and he would have had to find ways to combine his universalistic morality with the demands of nationhood.

First, the people's sense of collective identity had to be engrained into their minds: they became slaves in Egypt for three hundred years, and they had to experience humiliation and oppression at the hands of strange kings: they had to witness the miracles by which their God revealed Himself to them and released them from their bondage. Jews still consider their deliverance from slavery in Egypt the decisive event in their history. 'Everything in the Bible goes back to one thing,' writes Hyam Maccoby, 'that the people of Israel were once slaves in Egypt, and they experienced a great deliverance. This is the great event which Israel experienced as the irruption of the Divine into history... The one God of the universe, Creator of heaven and earth, "heard the cry" of the children of Israel, suffering under oppression, and intervened to help them.'[5]

There can be little doubt that this event impressed itself upon the Jews as the focal event of their history and, above all, as the starting-point for their emergence as a nation.

God raised a great prophet to whom he revealed his commandments and ordinances, and bade him to present them to the people of Israel assembled at the foot of Mount Sinai. Thus God's moral commandments were proclaimed to the whole community for the first time, and God addressed himself to his people on a new level of articulation: no longer in symbolic terms to selected individuals, but in clear and rational language comprehensible to all.

But right at the beginning of their emergence as a nation the Jews had to face the evils of nationhood. The Canaanites had to be conquered, their resistance overcome by war and bloodshed. But having determined that the Jews should have their own land, the land, moreover, in which Abraham dwelt and to whom God had promised that it would become a great nation for him and his descendants, the conquest became a matter of universal importance, a step in the fulfilment of God's purpose. Even so, the Israelites were enjoined not to exterminate the Canaanites but to drive them out:

'You shall not oppress a stranger; you know the heart of a stranger, for you were strangers in the land of Egypt.'

Exodus xxiii, 9.

Instead of battening on the defeated as a new ruling class (the usual role of conquerors), the Jews were to make a radically new start in the establishment of a nation of righteousness. (Many of the Canaanites in historical fact joined the community of the Israelites.)

4. THE RIGHTS OF MAN AND THE CONCEPT OF DIVINE JUSTICE

The laws of the Torah regarding man's relation to man constitute mankind's first 'Bill of Rights'. These laws boldly assert that man's freedom is his supreme right. He has the right to personal liberty, free speech and private property. His life and person are inviolate. Charges against him must be made in open court where he has a right to confront his accusers, cross-examine them and defend himself. The Torah recognises no class distinctions before the law. When it comes to justice there is no difference between patrician and plebeian, between the propertied and propertyless. As each man has innate in him the dignity of being the son of God, it makes no difference whether he is rich or poor, labourer or king. And justice must, therefore, apply to each man equally. This concept of the equality of human dignity before God is perfectly expressed in Hillel's dictums 'Love thy neighbour as thyself,' and 'Do not do unto others as you would not want them to do unto you.'

Moses was intent on abolishing slavery, but as he was not able in practice to do this, he introduced laws which were meant to ameliorate the indignity of slavehood and gradually abolish slavery entirely.[6] Laws applying to free men also applied to slaves, who had to be set free after seven years of servitude. Slave trading, as practised in the Christian world up till recently, was unthinkable to Jews. Kidnapping a Jew or Gentile, a white or black man, into slavery was an offence punishable by death. If a slave fled his master from one state to another, he could not be returned.

Lex talionis, the Roman name for the law of retaliation – an eye for an eye, a tooth for a tooth, a wound for a wound – has all too often been portrayed as a barbarous practice. Far from being barbarous, however, it was a 'law of restraint'. It was man's first step towards modern concepts of justice. In essence, it substituted public law for private vengeance, and served to prevent punishment in excess of the crime committed – the offender could not be made to pay for an eye with two. This limitation of punishment imposed by *lex talionis* led to the next step of paying compensation in money. We find this concept already embodied in earliest Mosaic law. Max I. Dimont compares this early legal system with that of the early Anglo-Saxons: 'While the Jews in the days of King David in 1000 BC had fully formalised civic laws, the Anglo-Saxons in AD 1000, i.e. two thousand years later, still practised ordeal by fire and trial by combat. These Anglo-Saxon legal notions held that innocence would be established if the accused survived walking through fire and that truth was on the side of the victor in an armed combat between two litigants. As those who were roasted alive, or were slain in trial-combat, never appealed their cases, it was natural for Anglo-Saxon intellectuals to deduce that divine justice had prevailed.'[7]

I should like to say here a few words about the concept of justice. The precept, 'Do not do unto others what you would not want them to do unto you', emphasises an awareness that other individuals share the same need for consideration and respect, and fear of being hurt, as oneself. This might be called justice founded on the universality of narcissistic sensibilities. The precept, 'Love thy neighbour as you love yourself', has its roots in mother's love for the child; it entails compassion and forgiveness in the same way as the mother loves her child without conditions and forgives 'trespasses'. This precept underlines man's desire to perpetuate mother's love into adulthood. Father's love, however, is conditional; it makes demands on the child to grow up, to be responsible for its actions; father's love implies the necessity of punishment for transgressions – punishment which should be commensurate with the transgression. The hurt inflicted on others must be met by the same hurt done to you.

Maternal and paternal aspects of justice apparently are in perennial conflict, yet both are necessary for the development and growth of a person and a culture. The former emphasises compassion and forgiveness, while the latter lays stress on responsibility and respect for others. The first focuses on mother's empathy with her child, the permanence of her love, while the latter stresses virtuous behaviour as a condition for being loved, resenting easy forgiveness for wrongdoing, for this can justify action harmful to others and reduce men to a state of childish irresponsibility. The father must establish guidelines and commandments of justice to teach to his children. He may feel compassion and forgiveness in his heart, yet will show that justice must be done, as it is a sign of his concern for all his children.

This sense of equality of all men before God the father, and the rule that no man should set himself above his fellow men, applies to kings and rulers of nations, for they too are men among men. Privileges of power must not lead them to forget the rights of their subjects, and they have a particular duty to restrain a disposition towards manic self-aggrandisement.

Nations have ascribed to their kings god-like qualities and worshipped them as gods; by making a human being into a god they allowed a man's limited mind and self-seeking interests to parade as ultimate justice and righteousness. The Jews were to have no such kings. Even Moses, the great prophet and founder of the Jewish nation, was prevented by God from entering the Promised Land lest he be worshipped as a divine king. The story of Moses' flirtation with divine power, as a maker of miracles, is told in his attempt to draw water from a rock. This story illustrates the disposition of great and powerful leaders to claim God-like qualities. Thus, in order to prevent Moses from becoming a focus of idolatry, he had to die before the Jews entered the Promised Land.

After many battles under the brilliant military leadership of Joshua, the Jews took possession of the Holy Land and divided it among the twelve tribes. These tribes were organised under the leadership of their elders in much the same way as the Greek city states were run by the *polis*. For there was only one God of wisdom and justice, and all decisions were made by men under his guidance and in keeping with the laws he had given to them:

And the people served the Lord all the days of Joshua, and all the days of the elders who outlived Joshua, who had seen all the great work which the Lord had done for Israel.

Judges ii, 7.

And God decided to give greater authority to the elders and to make them judges so that they could protect and guide the people with their learning, and to command greater influence over them, for it had appeared that the people constantly strayed from the path of righteousness while there was no authority over them.

5. UNIVERSALISM VERSUS NATIONALISM

When the great judge Samuel became old, the elders of Israel gathered together and said to Samuel:

'Behold, you are old and your sons do not walk in your ways; now appoint for us a king to govern us like all the nations.' But the thing displeased Samuel... and he prayed to the Lord. And the Lord said to Samuel, 'Hearken to the voice of the people in all that they say to you; for they have not rejected you, but they have rejected me from being king over them. According to all the deeds which they have done to me, from the day I brought them up out of Egypt even to this day, forsaking me and serving other gods, so they are also doing to you. Now then, hearken to their voice; only, you shall solemnly warn them, and show them the ways of the king who shall reign over them.'

So Samuel told all the words of the Lord to the people who were asking a king from him. He said: 'These will be the ways of the king who will reign over you: he will take your sons and appoint them to his chariots and to be his horsemen, and to run before his chariots; and he will appoint for himself commanders of thousands and commanders of fifties, and some to plough his ground and to reap his harvest, and to make his implements of war and the equipment of his chariots... He will take the best of your fields and vineyards and olive orchards and give them to his servants. He will take the tenth of your grain and of your vineyards and give it to his officers and to his servants... and he will take the best of your cattle and your asses, and put them to his work. He will take the tenth of your flocks, and you shall be his slaves. And in that day you will cry out because of your king, whom you have chosen for yourselves; but the Lord will not answer you in that day.'

But the people refused to listen to the voice of Samuel; and they said, 'No! but we will have a king over us, that we also may be like all the nations, and that our king may govern us and go out before us and fight our battles.' ... And the Lord said to Samuel, 'Hearken to their voice, and make them a king.' Samuel then said to the men of Israel, 'Go every man to his city.'

I. Samuel viii, 5-22.

God gave in to the clamour of his people and appointed them a king, no doubt once again disappointed about their continuing immaturity. He commanded Samuel, the last of the judges, to find a suitable ruler and to anoint him king over the people. With the anointment of Saul as first king of the Jews, the world's first kingship without divine right was initiated, for it was made clear that the Jewish king, unlike kings of other nations, was not a god nor has any divine origin attributed to him, and like all other men he was subject to the laws of the Torah. With a heavy heart God had to concede that his people were not yet mature enough to find sustenance and strength from the laws of Moses and from the spirit of righteousness which God had revealed to them. They had not sufficiently internalised His spirit, either as individuals or collectively as a nation, to be their internal guide and strength. His power and wisdom had not yet fully entered into their souls, and they needed a leader who would symbolise their craving for power and grandeur and under whose protection they could feel confident. (This weakness among men has continued unresolved through the ages, and transformed aspirations for universal justice into the rule of kings and tyrants. It has produced

Napoleon the king out of the spirit of liberty, equality and brotherhood, as it produced Stalin the tyrant out of the idea of the classless society.)

The abstract God was not yet convincing enough for the Jewish people to maintain them as a nation, and they wanted a king for whom they could fight and labour, to make him great and partake of his glory.

This retrogressive step in the development of the Jewish people was not to obliterate the presence of their God. The ultimate glory and righteousness would remain with Him. He continued to represent the supreme superego, and the kings – however great and powerful they might be – would still defer to God and depend on his help and support in their enterprises. God continues to represent a cosmic superego which reigns over kings and nations.

The covenant which he made with his people remains unbroken: his spirit is enshrined in the Ark of the Covenant, and the people of Israel take it with them wherever they go. In peace and in war it is the focus of their identity and, even if their nation is conquered and kings are killed, the words of the Torah remain as a sacred and eternal affirmation of their faith and their identity; amidst persecution and poverty the Scrolls of the Torah convey to them the glory of God.

Even if their cities and homes, shrines and temples, are destroyed, they retain their identity as a people, for the words of God are forever, and are impervious to the vicissitudes of the world. (Even in the death camps they remembered the words and wrote them down and rallied round them. And through the two thousand years of the diaspora, the rabbis debated the true meaning of the words of God, wrote down the interpretations of the interpretations, and the books of the Talmud were taught in schools, and the schools as synagogues became the centre of the community.)

In those early days, when they embarked on the path of kingship and nationhood, God determined that the existence of his people would not depend on territory and the life of the king, for these are transient and subject to complex interaction and accidents of history. Kings, moreover, are particularly vulnerable to manic fantasies. They want to usurp God and take his place, and be like him. They want to acquire omnipotence and omniscience and present themselves to the people as gods. Indeed, we can say that the manic cravings of man, exemplified by kings and nation states, represent the manic cycle of the manic-depressive syndrome. The downfall of kings and nations represents punishment by the superego for wanting to kill the father and take his place – Adam's perennial sin – in the same way as the depressive phase of manic-depressive individuals represents their guilt and punishment by the superego. In the mythology of the Jews, it is history as an instrument of God's will which enacts the punishment for the manic presumption of nations and the king's usurpation of God's power. There is no end to the downfall of nations and killings of kings which are seen as punishments by God – the depressive phase of the manic disposition of kingship and nationalism.

God, of course, foresaw the development of this pathology once a king was appointed to rule over His people, so he appointed prophets to act as His spokesmen. They would remind the people of their covenant with God, and they would uphold the laws of his righteousness. They would mediate between God and his people, they would pronounce his judgments, and expose their errors and condemn their misdeeds. They would make the people remember his commandments of moral righteousness by which nations are to be judged. (In this way the Jews showed how the dilemma which faced Plato could be solved. Plato wanted the philosopher to be king but realised that philosophers would be reluctant to take on this duty.)

The two greatest kings of the Jews, David and Solomon, were imbued with God's spirit – one as an artist, singer and poet, and the other as a philosopher. But still they were subject to the judgement of prophets, who regarded them as fallible human beings, pointing out their errors and leading them back to the path of righteousness. 'The human rulers of Israel are chosen, accepted or tolerated by God, but they remain subordinate to him and they are judged by the degree of fidelity to the indissoluble covenant between Yahweh and his people.'[8]

The fact that the king was equal with the poorest in the land and subject to the laws of God emphasised the equality of all men and contributed to the idea that the individual was important in himself and not merely as part of a social group. Thus his importance and his dignity as a person was conferred on him by his relationship to God which overrides his status in the social hierarchy.

When the spirit of God descended upon a man he felt called upon to speak His words, whether he be prince or shepherd, rich or poor; he would consider it as his duty to be a judge to his people. The prestige he acquired as a prophet put him in a powerful position to comment on, or criticize, the behaviour of kings and governments, or Israelite society as a whole. As the vehicle of a message from God he enjoyed considerable immunity, even if his message gave offence, since only the most ruthless rulers dare to act against such a man. As early as the reign of David, the prophet Nathan was able to rebuke the king for adultery and murder, and caused him to repent of his sins.

'Why have you despised the word of the Lord to do what is evil in His sight?' ... And David said to Nathan: 'I have sinned against the Lord.'

II. Samuel xii, 9; 13.

38

And after David had repented and admitted the evil of his action and submitted to God's judgment, Nathan said to him:

'The Lord also has put away your sin; you shall not die.'
II. Samuel xii, 13.

In the following century, the prophet Elijah was the mouth-piece for the condemnation of land-snatching perpetrated by Ahab and Jezebel, and Elisha was instrumental in bringing about a dynastic revolution.

By the middle of the eighth century BC, the prophet Amos was criticising many aspects of life in Palestine. He condemned such matters as brutality in war and economic oppression of the poor.

Under David and his son, Solomon, Israel became a major power in the Middle East. At Solomon's death (922 BC), the northern tribes broke away to form a separate kingdom, Israel, while the southern tribes remained in David's dynasty as the kingdom of Judah. These kingdoms maintained commercial, military and diplomatic contacts with their neighbours, particularly the Phoenicians and the Arameans.

In the mid-ninth century BC Israel had its first military encounter with Assyria, an expanding state, which in the second half of the eighth century BC spread out to make all the states of Syria and Palestine its vassals. Assyria conquered the kingdom of Israel and brought it to an end in 722 BC, but the Davidic dynasty continued in Judah until 586 BC, when that kingdom was extinguished by the Babylonians under Nebuchadnezzar.

In five fiery sermons the prophet Amos forged the universalistic framework of prophetic philosophy. It was, however, his contemporary Isaiah who became the chief exponent of the unity of moral and political dimensions of God's commandments. Just as Abraham was the founder of the chosen people, as Moses gave the Jews their laws and enabled them to become a nation, so it was Isaiah who gave the Jews their universalistic message of a future brotherhood of men, a vision which they were to convey to the world. Born c. 760 BC, Isaiah addressed himself in the most powerful language to the social ills of his time and extended the principles of monotheism even to international political relations. His prophecies convey God's love for his people and his vision of them as the teachers of humanity as well as his outrage against their iniquities. He does not merely chastise the powerful but addresses himself to the people in their collective responsibility for transgressions and injustices.

Isaiah was possibly the greatest of the poet seers and at the same time a man of action, a statesman of unerring judgement. His experience of being called by God moreover gave an incandescent quality to his genius. 'The majesty of his description of Yahweh's coming in judgement is superb... If, to be a genius of the first rank, a man must be at once a creative artist and a man of affairs, Isaiah must be accorded his place among the select few. And his was genius heightened by utter consecration to the service of God.' [9] And we can also hold a man to be a genius of the first order if he has, like Isaiah, come to exercise a lasting influence, and had his ideas accepted as the foundation for the moral and political concepts of mankind.

> Hear, O heavens, and give ear, O earth;
>   for the Lord has spoken:
> 'Sons have I reared and brought up,
>   but they have rebelled against me.
> The ox knows its owner, and the ass its master's crib; but
>   Israel does not know, my people does not understand.'
>
> *Isaiah* i, 2-3.

> The Lord has taken his place to contend,
>   he stands to judge his people.

The Lord enters into judgment with the elders and princes
of his people: 'It is you who have devoured the vineyard,
    the spoil of the poor is in your houses.
What do you mean by crushing my people, by grinding
    the face of the poor?' says the Lord God of hosts.

Isaiah iii, 13-15.

Woe to those who decree iniquitous decrees, and the writers
  who keep writing oppression, to turn aside the needy from
  justice and to rob the poor of my people of their right,
    that widows may be their spoil, and that
    they may make the fatherless their prey!
  What will you do on the day of punishment,
in the storm which will come from afar? To whom will
you flee for help, and where will you leave your wealth?

Isaiah x, 1-3.

'Come now, let us reason together, says the Lord:
though your sins are like scarlet, they shall be as white as snow;
though they are red like crimson, they shall become like wool.
    If you are willing and obedient, you shall eat
the good of the land; but if you refuse and rebel, you shall be
devoured by the sword; for the mouth of the Lord has spoken.'

Isaiah i, 18-20.

For out of Zion shall go forth the law, and the word of the
  Lord from Jerusalem. He shall judge between the nations,
and shall decide for many peoples; and they shall beat their
swords into ploughshares, and their spears into pruning hooks;
    nation shall not lift up sword against nation,
    neither shall they learn war any more.

Isaiah ii, 3-4.

'They shall build houses and inhabit them; they shall
plant vineyards and eat their fruit. They shall not build
and another inhabit; they shall not plant and another eat.'

Isaiah lxv, 21.

'Rejoice with Jerusalem, and be glad for her, all you who love
    her; rejoice with her in joy, all you who mourn over her;
that you may suck and be satisfied with her consoling breasts,
that you may drink deeply with delight from the abundance
        of her glory.'
    For thus says the Lord: 'Behold, I will extend prosperity
to her like a river, and the wealth of the nations like an over-
flowing stream, and you shall suck, you shall be carried upon
her hip, and dandled upon her knees. As one whom his mother
    comforts, so I will comfort you; you shall be comforted
    in Jerusalem. You shall see, and your heart shall rejoice...'
                                            Isaiah lxvi, 10-14.

In the last two passages, we can see the emergence of a maternalistic morality governed by the love of the mother, depicted
by Jerusalem as the daughter-wife of God and the mother of
mankind.

When one hundred and fifty years after the fall of Israel,
Jerusalem was overwhelmed by the Babylonians and the kingdom of Judah destroyed, the Jews were spiritually prepared;
they could not avert the military disaster but they had the spiritual strength to prevent it from destroying them as a nation.
With the charismatic power imbued into them by the Book of
Deuteronomy, their Bible, and with the ideas supplied to them
by the prophets, the Jews of Judah possessed a deep sense of
their own collective identity to survive in exile.

Under the impetus of the prophetic guidelines the exiled Jews
innovated ideas on Babylonian soil. Instead of a temple for a
priesthood cult, they built synagogues for popular devotion, and
instead of sacrifices they offered prayers. Thus freed from priesthood, temple and sacrifice, the Jews could set up synagogues
everywhere, with the Torah as the symbol of God's presence.
So the survival of Judaism in exile had been assured.

But the man who above all others held the presence of God

before the Jewish mind was the prophet Jeremiah. He addressed his people during the four decades before the Babylonian conquest of 586 BC with a directness and power unmatched by any of his contemporaries; it was he, more than any other, who gave expression to a faith and hope and indeed a theology which made it possible for Judah to survive the disaster of the nation's fall, the destruction of the temple, and the end of the Davidic dynasty.

It was at the turn of the sixth century BC that the calamitous events occurred which in a few years were to blot out Judah as a nation-state. They ended with the road to exile and forcible removal to Babylon.

6. THE EXILE IN BABYLON

In the year 586 BC Nebuchadnezzar arrived with a strong army from Babylon and began his assault against the nation, much weakened after the previous defeat by the Babylonians in 597 BC. The Chaldean divisions of infantry, fast cavalry and charioteers smashed all resistance and conquered city after city. Except for the capital Jerusalem, and the frontier fortresses of Lachish and Azekah in the south, the whole land was finally subdued. These three fortified towns however were determined to fight until the end. After the Babylonian armies stormed Lachish and Azekah, only Jerusalem remained, and the whole weight of the Babylon war-machine was now directed against it. Jerusalem was plundered and the royal palace and the temple were set on fire. The city walls and fortifications were razed to the ground. Nebuchadnezzar erased the royal house of David which had reigned for four hundred years.

But Jeremiah foresaw the destruction of the kingdom:
Behold... says the Lord... I will make the cities of Judah
a desolation, without inhabitant.

For he had commanded them to make a proclamation of liberty:

> that every one should set free his Hebrew slaves, male and female, so that no one should enslave a Jew, his brother... they obeyed and set them free. But afterward they turned around and took back the male and female slaves they had set free, and brought them into subjection...

The word of the Lord came to Jeremiah:

> I made a covenant with your fathers when I brought them out of the land of Egypt... but then you profaned my name when each of you took back his male and female slaves, whom you had set free... and you brought them into subjection... You have not obeyed me by proclaiming liberty, everyone to his brother and to his neighbour; behold, I proclaim to you liberty to the sword, to pestilence, and to famine.'
>
> *Jeremiah* xxxiv, 22; 8-13, 16-17.

So Jeremiah instructed His people to go into exile, and:

> Build houses and live in them; plant gardens and eat their produce... that you may be increased there and not decrease. And seek the peace of the city where I have sent you into exile... When seventy years are completed for Babylon, I will visit you, and I will fulfil to you my promise and bring you back to Jerusalem.
>
> *Jeremiah* xxix, 5-10.

It seems that God once again despaired over his people's inability to take his words to their hearts, or, to put it into a more correct and mundane way, the writers of the Bible wanted to emphasise men's perennial difficulty of resolving the conflict between the call of king and nation and the call of justice and human brotherhood. (And it must never be forgotten that the Jewish people are meant to be an example to mankind, both of its aspirations and its frailties, a mirror, as it were, held up to men in which they can recognise themselves.)

God no doubt regretted his decision to allow the people to

have kings to rule over them, thereby saddling them with conflicts they could not resolve. For kingship and nationhood produce hierarchic systems of authority which encourage the desire
for power and obsession with manic fantasies on the one hand,
and oppression on the other.

The psychic processes of the Oedipus complex which demand
the restitution of the slain father into a powerful king and, at
the same time, a foreign enemy upon whom the aggressive
drives can be displaced, were of course well known to God; for
the Oedipal conflicts not only produce kings and paranoid fears
of other nations, worship of authority, sacrificial dispositions and
warfare, endless bloodshed and injustice, but also visions of
peace and justice among men. God, who intended to help men
resolve this conflict and realise their vision, conceived a plan
whereby the Jewish nation would be destroyed, and they would
learn to live without a king and without the institutions of nationhood; he sent them into exile where he hoped they would
learn the essence of his message: not nationalism but righteousness among men.

'For I know the plans I have for you, says the Lord, plans for
welfare and not for evil, to give you a future and a hope.'
                                                    Jeremiah xxix, 11.

The exile in Babylon turned out to be far less harsh and
oppressive than that experienced in Egypt. Those who took
Jeremiah's advice as their guide, got on quite well, some indeed
very well. There is the example of a Jewish family who started
a business firm, which I cannot forbear to mention: 'Murashu
& Sons'. We read on their business documents in clay: 'International Bank – Insurance, conveyancing, loans, personal and
real estate. Head Office: Nippur – branches everywhere'. This
family had done well for themselves in Nippur since 587 BC

when they left Jerusalem. Their firm still stood for something in Mesopotamia even in the Persian era, some two hundred years later. The 'books' of 'Murashu & Sons' are full of detailed information about the lives of the exiles, such as their names, their occupations and their property.

From these records and others which have been unearthed recently, we can have a glimpse of the lives of the exiled Jews. They became established as merchants, copper- and silversmiths, jewellers, shopkeepers and farmers. However, there was a significant shift from their old occupations as peasants, cattle-breeders and craftsmen, to commerce. The law of Israel had made no provision for commerce. It appeared as an alien occupation. The word Canaanite was for them synonymous with shopkeepers, merchants, bankers – people whom the prophets had vigorously castigated for their sins.

> He is a merchant, the balances of deceit are in his hand, he loves to oppress.
>
> *Hosea* xii, 7.

The change to commercial professions was no doubt encouraged by the high degree of literacy among Jews, and it made them at home in large cities within which they could build houses and form communities and devote themselves to their religious services. It gave them cohesion and continuity.

The Israelites could not have chosen a better training college. Babylon, as an international centre of trade, industry and commerce, was the great school for the cities and capitals of the whole world. The metropolis, whose ruins after 2,500 years still betray its ancient power and glory, had no equal in the ancient world. [10]

But however much the Jews may have sought 'the peace of the city' and found it, however much they may have learned in the cities of Babylon which would profit future generations, their yearning for their distant homeland left them no peace. They could not forget the city of David, their beloved Jerusalem.

By the waters of Babylon, there we sat down and wept, when we remembered Zion.

Psalm cxxxvii, 1.

These were no empty words, for most of them, once the opportunity arose, set out on the difficult journey home.

The opportunity to return came when Cyrus, the king of Persia, conquered Babylon in 539 BC. He gave the order which allowed the Jews not merely to return to their homeland but 'that the expenses for their journey be paid out of the king's house. And also let the golden and silver vessels of the house of God, which Nebuchadnezzar took out of the temple which is at Jerusalem and brought into Babylon, be restored and brought back to the temple... and put them in the house of God' (*Ezra* vi, 4-5).

In the spring of 537 BC, after long preparations, a large caravan set out for the old homeland. The efforts of the returned exiles were for many years confined almost exclusively to re-building the temple at Jerusalem. Building started in October 520 BC, and by March 515 BC it was complete. However, the Jews knew full well that the days of the monarchy had gone forever and that only the solidarity of their religious community would guarantee the continued existence of the nation in face of whatever political developments might be in store. With this end in view, they made the Holy City the centre of Jewry, both for the Jews living in the homeland and for those scattered throughout the world. They abdicated from efforts to make an impact on the affairs of nations during subsequent centuries. (We must bear in mind that the building of the temple was made possible by the contributions from prosperous Jews in Babylonia, Rome and Egypt.)

With Persian approval the law of God became the law of Israel, indeed, of Jews everywhere, as the Book of Ezra clearly indicates.

It has often been noted that despite the relative peace after the return from exile there was a complete absence of large buildings, fine palaces or public monuments. Many observers interpret this state of affairs as signs of poverty at that time. It would, however, be more correct to consider this absence of great buildings as due to an absence of an aristocratic elite which traditionally employs a large part of the nation's wealth to build monuments for its self-glorification. Moreover, the injunction against idol worship, against glorification of kings or self-glorification by means of graven images, would have been observed after the return from exile; for as we have said, exile meant the abolition of kingship in Judah. And when the Jews came back from Babylon they resolved to dispense with kings and worship of nationalism.

Even the temple was not the same as before; in their zeal to turn to the fundamental faith embodied by the Mosaic laws, the Jews, mainly under the inspiration of Ezra and Nehemiah, decreed that the five books of Moses should be read aloud in every synagogue at special intervals each week. They also decreed that special interpreters should be at hand to explain difficult Hebrew passages, because most people no longer spoke Hebrew but Aramaic. The task of explaining the Hebrew text of the Torah was entrusted to a group of men called sofers, literally 'bookmen', but better known as scribes. And these scribes went beyond giving explanations of difficult passages and obscure laws, but began to interpret their meaning in respect to contemporary problems and practical needs. They gradually transformed themselves from being explainers to interpreters of the Torah, and developed a new science of interpretation that came to be known as midrash or 'exposition'. The people of Judah determined to find their sense of national and religious identity in the words of God, in the study and interpretation of their Scripture and of the laws contained therein. They transferred the narcissistic libido, forever trying to find symbolic representation in material objects – 'graven images' – to the written and spoken word; the word would thus acquire magic powers, the embodiment of God's Spirit and become the focus of worship among the Jews.

We can see some examples of the importance given to the written word in the colophon, in which the artist produced imaginative forms out of letters, sometimes taking the shapes of animals and landscapes. For instance, colophons of a bible written in Spain in AD1300 took the form of multi-headed birds composed of lines of tiny writing. Many such exuberant expressions by artistic scribes have appeared in medieval bibles, reflecting a love for the written word combined with artistic imagery and we can assume they had their counterpart, indeed, origins, in the centuries of the post-exilic civilisation of Judea. The term, 'the People of the Book', is thus wholly appropriate for the Jews. The scribe was for them a sacred artist, in some respects, a holy man; he was highly respected and received with honour in their far-flung settlements in Egypt, Mesopotamia, Greece and Rome. We are here reminded of the emergence of the humanists during the European Renaissance, the man of letters, who held, in the words of Leon Battista Alberti, that: 'He who has learnt everything is nowhere a stranger; even if he be robbed of his fortune and without friends, he is yet a citizen of every country and can fearlessly despise the changes of fortune. Wherever a learned man fixes his seat, there is home.' And there can be no higher accolade for the Jewish nation than being the home of the learned.

Study of the Holy Scripture would thus be a chief form of their worship; interpretation and commentaries on such interpretations would be their ritual. These activities were called the oral tradition as distinct from the authority of the written Bible, and eventually they were written down and codified in the Mishnah which became a central part of the Talmud. The priests, or Sadducees, who were generally tied to the pre-exilic Judaism, in the main rejected the oral tradition, the interpretations of the Bible and the application and adaptation of its laws and requirements to contemporary life.

The Sadducees considered themselves as the guardians of the written words of the Torah which did not require any further elaboration or interpretation, being unquestionable authority, while the Pharisees determined to apply their intellect to further elaboration and a deeper understanding of the significance of the words.

In the rift between Sadducees and Pharisees we see the opposition between worship dominated by ritualistic obsessionalism and the expansive application of the intellect, between those to whom worship means the observation of ritual and those to whom worship means communion with the spirit and intention which lie behind the words, between orthodoxy and liberalism. The question at what point truth becomes dogma and worship an obsession is, of course, a perennial problem. It is the difference between a truth that represents a repressive superego and men's submission to it and a truth that stands for the ego's quest to achieve intellectual maturity and personal dignity in relation to the superego. (There can be no doubt that the latter corresponds more closely to God's intentions, as we have seen earlier, and is repeatedly emphasised in the Talmud.) This conflict between dogma and reason led to a dramatic confrontation that became a watershed in the history of Western civilisation. But of this later.

7. THE CONQUESTS OF ALEXANDER THE GREAT

After about two hundred years, the Persian domination was brought to an end by the conquests of Alexander the Great (333 BC). The Bible has little to say about these events, as indeed about the whole period of Greek supremacy for almost one hundred and fifty years. But Flavius Josephus, the Jewish historian, gives an account of the campaign of the victorious Greeks through Syria and Palestine at this time. After the capture of the fortress of Gaza, he says Alexander the Great came to Jerusalem. The people and Jaddua, the High Priest, received him with great ceremony. Alexander offered sacrifices in the temple and granted the people favours. Jerusalem and the province of Judah seem to have submitted to their new masters without any more ado. The visit of Alexander to Jerusalem may only be a legend, but it bears witness to the fact that the Greek conquerors tolerated the way of life of Judah. It was unmolested as a religious community.

Egypt welcomed Alexander as a liberator during the winter of 332-331 BC. He founded the city of Alexandria which was destined for the role of the metropolis of the new age. It quickly blossomed into the centre of a new intellectual life which attracted the best minds of the Greek and oriental world within its ambit and came to play a decisive role in the preservation of Greek and Jewish culture. At its foundation, Alexander issued instructions which were of the highest significance. He guaranteed to the Jews the same rights as were accorded to his own countrymen. This provision, carried on by his successors, led to Alexandria becoming subsequently one of the great centres of Jewish culture and philosophy.

In face of the growing influence of Greek civilisation, the Jews kept themselves to themselves. On the death of Alexander, the Bible comments wryly:

> So Alexander died and his servants tried to rule everyone in
> his stead, and after his death they all put crowns upon them-
> selves; so did their sons after many years: and evils were multi-
> plied in the world.
>
> *I. Maccabees* i, 7-9.

Can we not detect here the sophisticated reflection of a people
who had long ago dispensed with the power-seeking compulsions of kinghood?

The conflict between Alexander's successors resulted in a
division of his empire into three kingdoms: the kingdom of
Macedonia in northern Greece, the kingdom of the Seleucids
which extended through Asia Minor and Syria to the borders
of India with Antioch as its capital, and the Ptolemaic kingdom
of Egypt with Alexandria as its capital.

Judah was attached to the Ptolemies, and their far-sighted and
tolerant rulers protected the country for more than one hundred
years. Then the Seleucids of Antioch pushed their way south-
wards and took over Palestine in 190 BC, and Judah came once
more under a new sovereignty. Gradually the influence of the
Greek attitude of mind which had been infiltrating since Alexander's victorious campaigns became more and more powerful and particularly the philosophy of late Hellenism began to
exercise its influence upon the Jews. Moreover, the Seleucids
were not as tolerant and liberal as their predecessors.

King Antiochus IV, called Epiphanes, plundered and des-
ecrated the temple in the year 168 BC. Never before, neither
under the Assyrians nor under the Babylonians, had Israel received such a blow as the edict issued by Antiochus Epiphanes,
by which he hoped to crush and destroy the faith of Israel:

> And the king sent letters by the hand of messengers into Je-
> rusalem and the cities of Judah, that they should follow laws
> strange to the land.
>
> *I. Maccabees* i, 44

The worship of Olympian Zeus was set up in the temple of God. 'For taking part in any Jewish religious ceremonies, the traditional sacrifices, the Sabbath or circumcision, the penalty was death. The Holy Scriptures were destroyed. This was the first thoroughgoing religious persecution in history. But Israel gave the world an example of how a nation that refuses to be untrue to itself can and must react to a violation of its conscience of this kind.'[11] The Jewish people rose up against these outrages, they took up arms against the desecrators of their faith, and the Maccabean revolt succeeded in re-establishing their liberty of worship and their religious communities.

However, the Maccabees proceeded to demand political independence as well as freedom of religion. After an incredible twenty-five years' struggle against an enemy one hundred times its size, Judea won, and the Maccabees established the Hasmonean dynasty on the throne of Judah. Its frontiers were extended until they almost completely covered the area previously occupied by the united kingdoms of Israel and Judah, until in 63 BC Pompey, the Roman general, marched through Assyria into Palestine.

The Romans captured Jerusalem and brought the Jewish nation under their control. Thus after less than one hundred years the independence of Judah, achieved with much difficulty and considerable heroism, had fallen victim to Rome.

We have noted in the unfolding of Jewish history a dialectic interaction between divine inspiration, which we may call the impact of the transcendental, and the spirit of tribalism extended to nationhood. When the Jews of old insisted on having a king, God had to accede to their nationalistic impulses but gave them prophets to uphold an awareness of their mission; through the prophets the voice of the transcendental, the universal spirit, continued to speak to men. After the Babylonian exile the Jews set out to mould their society according to the laws of God but could not insulate themselves from the turmoil of expansionist nations all round them. They fought for their independence in the Maccabean wars, but once again succumbed to the desire for kingship, and the priests and Sadducees not only gave whole-hearted support to the royal establishment of the Roman Empire but became an integral part of it. There were no more prophets, however, to keep the ethics of universalism alive; the Pharisees and rabbis took the place of prophets, but they no longer spoke with prophetic voices.

We see here a parallel with the ideal of the Greek philosopher, but while the philosopher devoted his intellect to the discovery of truth, the rabbis applied their rational faculties to the clarification and understanding of the Torah. It was not the truth that needed to be discovered but correct understanding of the Scriptures which contain the truth. Knowledge of the law and its correct application was the sign of wisdom; the rabbis held that wisdom and the ultimate truth is provided by God, and considered themselves to be merely expositors of the law, explainers and interpreters of the revealed truth.

The indissoluble unity between faith and learning was a fundamental and dominant concept of the rabbis. Only pious learning is wisdom and infinitely superior to learning without faith, not to speak of the clever sinner. Cleverness without faith is equal to craftiness and malevolence. The law without religion, therefore, is not to be trusted, legalism without ethics no more than a stratagem that can be upheld for the promotion of evil. The rabbis became lawyers revealing in practical matters the wisdom and will of God, the unity of theology and jurisdiction. The culture and learning of the rabbis represented the ideal of the Jewish people, an ideal that made life worthwhile.

Individuals like Hillel, Gamaliel and Jochanan commanded great respect, and their learning was considered the pinnacle of wisdom. However, there emerged considerable differences between them, even leading to schisms in the interpretations of the law. While they all shared the conviction that it was the learned man's privilege and, indeed, his duty to educe principles of justice from scriptural foundations and to elaborate the laws of the Torah in order to make them applicable to the affairs of men, some applied the method of exegesis more rigidly and made their judgments more dogmatic than others. Among those who aimed towards the exercise of reason rather than dogma Hillel stood out above all others.

He came to Jerusalem in order to continue his studies in the advanced academies, principally of the great expositors Shemaiah and Avtalyon. His erudition and skill in argument was early recognised, and he was made head of the temple commission. His sophisticated hermeneutical principles were of special significance, laying the foundation for a scientific formulation of the new Mishnah.

The demands of the Pharisee intellectuals to define divine laws by reason and to make logical deductions from the written law of the Torah had to be met, and Hillel did this with his seven rules. They provided the groundwork and guide for the correct application of divine laws to the requirements of practical reality through the use of logic. He was a champion of the liberal school and attempted to free the law from a blind worship of the word; he gave the greatest possible scope for the exercise of freedom and compassion in human affairs. His best known saying was: 'What is hateful to you do not do to your fellow men: this is the whole law and the rest is commentary.' It was based on the biblical precept: 'Thou shalt love thy neighbour as thyself.'

However, the Mishnah and the work of its great expositors was viewed with misgiving by the Sadducees who were tied to the administration of temple ritual sacrifice and the written word of the Torah. They were supporters of the monarchy (especially as in the late Hasmonean period the institutions of monarchy and high priesthood were combined). When the Romans turned Judea into a Roman province and abolished the monarchy, the Sadducees, always on the side of the ruling establishment, accepted positions of authority under Roman rule. The high priest was a Roman appointee and was regarded by the Pharisees, as a whole, with contempt. [12]

8. PHARISEES AND SADDUCEES

There emerged a situation when the Pharisees, who were recognised by the people as their religious leaders, had to oppose the Sadducees' party, which on the one hand upheld a strict and conservative orthodoxy and on the other hand was prepared to serve a foreign master and co-operate in the subjection of the Jewish nation; in the hands of the Sadducees Scripture had become deadened, the holy words devoid of fresh inspiration and deprived of intellectual and moral meaning.

Just as in the life of an individual the various stages of the libido strive for primacy, that is, influence upon the ego, so they compete for supremacy in the life of a culture: the destructive Thanatos-ridden forces versus the creative life-affirming forces; the angry and jealous desires against the desires for love and friendship; and compulsive rituals against the freedom to activate men's spiritual and intellectual faculties. It is the last of these conflicts which especially plays an important role in the battle for supremacy, both between cultures and within a culture; it came to a head during those critical times of Jewish history.

Regression to obsessive levels of worship occurs in practically all religions and cultures, and can be summed up by the term 'orthodoxy' and its twin, 'dogmatism'. The great ideas and poetic images that have given birth to religions and ideologies are soon overtaken by the compulsions of ritual worship:

Judaism, Christianity, Islam as well as science and socialism have become a battleground between the regressive imperatives of orthodoxy on the one hand and liberalism on the other, between dogmatic adherence to the letter and the free exercise of spiritual and rational faculties in the pursuit of an ideal.

We might say that once a culture regresses to orthodoxy a kind of binary system begins to operate: clean and unclean; pure and impure; correct and incorrect; trustworthy and suspicious. Orthodoxy thus is a particularly fertile breeding ground for social and religious paranoia. [13]

(There is a profound difference between the binary opposites operating in orthodoxy and dialectics. While in the former the opposites remain absolute and immovable, in the latter the opposites between thesis and antithesis evolve into a new category – synthesis. While the first is static, the second is a vehicle for progress.)

There is no doubt that obsessive ritualism is a particular characteristic of priesthood. Priests are in the first place sacrificers, appointed to receive from the people gifts to the gods, gifts by which people hope to be redeemed and still the gods' anger. The satisfaction of the gods depends on the skills by which the priests carry out their sacrificial ceremonials. Any deviation from the pre-ordained ritual would disturb the gods and thus evoke anxiety. Orthodox Jews, however, not only employ priests to fulfil sacrificial ceremonials on their behalf but consider themselves to be a nation of priests and are therefore obliged to engage in ceremonials of purification and sacrifice during the course of their lives. Not only the priests but every orthodox individual must engage in certain rituals and arrange his life around them.

On the level of literacy attained by the Jews the written word acquired ritual significance. Priestly orthodoxy demands that devotion to the word adopts ritual form in which no letter, no comma, must be lost or neglected. Thus the priestly keepers of the written word converted it into a fetish, indeed, a graven image. They have taken the spirit from it, it has ceased to be a stimulus to the intellect, and its meaning, revealing the spirit and purpose of God, has become lost.

The rabbis, on the other hand, have upheld, as we have seen, men's privilege and duty to consider the written word as a stimulus for intellectual inquiry, in order to educe the richness of its meanings and acquire a deeper understanding of God's mind. (Einstein said that he is not merely concerned whether a particular mathematical formula is correct, but that he wants to understand God's mind.) The rabbis of old considered the Jewish people sufficiently mature to encounter God's messages as intelligent persons; moreover, they upheld their right to arrive at decisions about the correctness of an interpretation by means of debate and democratic vote, even ruling God 'out of order' on a certain occasion when he wanted to intervene in their deliberations: 'And God laughed and said: "My children are growing up."' We might call this aspect of rabbinic learning their humanism, as against the totalitarian outlook of the priests. But it could happen that even priests were humanists at times and rabbis orthodox-totalitarians. On the whole, however, the schism was between priestly orthodoxy and rabbinic humanism. Their conflict was brought to a head by the appointment of the high priest by the Romans. Thus the Pharisee rabbis were forced not only to fight against the Roman occupation but also against their own priests whom they regarded as traitors. When their very existence was at stake the Jewish people felt themselves betrayed by their priestly leaders. Despite repeated revolts against Roman occupying forces the chances of freeing their country from a ruthless occupation must have appeared slender indeed.

The Romans' lack of respect for the Jewish religion, their frequent incursions into the Holy of Holies, the high level of

Graeco-Roman culture which for many years past made increasing inroads on Judea, must have produced a deep sense of desperation among many Jews. Some, such as the Zealots, resolved to fight Rome by the sword, and hoped to initiate the kingdom of God – not the rule of kings but of God – and invoked his help in this struggle; others prayed for a miraculous intervention by God, so hoping that he would destroy the Romans in a conflagration, thus showing his power not only to the Jews but to the world.

It was a time of desperation, not untouched by hysteria, and there were many would-be Messiahs. It was in this situation that a teacher appeared who was to change the face of the world. He claimed to be the Messiah and eventually he came to be worshipped as a God. His name was Yeshua, and he became known as Jesus.

Notes to Judaism.

[1] *See* Hyam Maccoby: Section I, 2: 'The Bible', in *The Jewish World – Revelation, Prophecy and History* (Ed. Elie Kedourie), Thames & Hudson, 1979, p. 53.

[2] *See* Saggs, H. W. F: *The Babylonians*, Macmillan Publishers Ltd / The Folio Society, 1962, 1988, p. 57 and p. 422.

[3] *See* Feiler, Bruce: *Abraham – In Search of the Father of Civilisation*, Piatkus, 2002, p. 28 and pp. 33-4.

[4] Sigmund Freud: *Moses and Monotheism*, S. E. XXIII – 2: 3, 6.

[5] Hyam Maccoby: Section I, 2: 'The Bible', in *The Jewish World*, Thames & Hudson, 1979, p. 54.

[6] The enslavement of members of a nation conquered in wars was a universal practice taken for granted and unquestioned as the norm, and handed down by ancient tradition.

[7] Max I. Dimont: *The Indestructible Jews*, New American Library, 1971, pp. 46-47.

[8] Roland de Vaux: *Ancient Israel – Its Life and Institutions*, Darton, Longman & Todd, 1973, Chapter IV, 7, p. 99.

[9] *See* article on Isaiah by C. R. North in *The Interpreter's Dictionary of the Bible*, Vol. 2, Abingdon Press, 1962, p. 733.

[10] Werner Keller: *The Bible as History*, Hodder & Stoughton, 1956, p. 283, and p. 285.

[11] *Ibid.* pp. 315-316.

[12] Hyam Maccoby: *Revolution in Judaea – Jesus and the Jewish Resistance*, Orbach & Chambers, 1973, Chapter VI, p. 92.

[13] It is interesting to note that adherents of structuralism have taken their model for the human mind from cybernetics and early computer logic, applying it to the interpretation of cultures. Those of Levi-Strauss' followers such as Edmund Leach and Jacob Neusner who have subjected Jewish religion to structuralist analysis, stress Jewish orthodoxy dominated by ritual purity, finding in such religious observances, and certain aspects of Talmudic legalism, a rich field to prove their binary theories. However they are grossly mistaken in adopting their model to the whole of the Jewish religion; they have no eye at all for the much wider dimensions of thought and symbolism which are of supreme importance not only in Judaism but in all cultures.

PART 2   *Christianity*

Christianity

1. JESUS OF NAZARETH: RABBI OR GOD?

There is no end to the books written about Jesus and the origins of Christianity. Most of these books are obviously expressions of Christian belief, manipulating the facts in order to promote their faith: 'The Gospels themselves provide the fullest and most instructive examples of fervent embellishment of, and interpolation into, historical fact.'[1]

The Gospels as well as a large majority of Christian books, including works of Christian scholarship, barely mention the Roman occupation, a fact that dominated the life of the country and the condition of its people, nor do they show the Jewish nature of Jesus' teaching and its continuity with the Pharisee tradition.

It is only in recent years that the Jewishness of Jesus has been made clear by such writers as S. G. F. Brandon, James Parkes, E. P. Sanders, Paul Winter, C. H. Dodd, Hugh Schonfield, Geza Vermes and Hyam Maccoby. It is now possible to form a fairly clear view of the historical conditions which gave rise to the teaching of the Rabbi Yeshua of Nazareth and its continuity with rabbinic thought, both in its content and form.

His use of parables, which was treated as a tortuous problem by Christian scholars, is shown by Dodd and Maccoby to be the traditional method of presentation used by the rabbis, while their intellectual content expresses well-established rabbinic doctrine.

There is also little doubt that the young rabbi expressed the Pharisaic point of view with great clarity and force. By his brilliance as a speaker, his impassioned advocacy of rabbinic convictions and his powers as a healer, by his remorseless attack upon the priests and Sadducees combined with his charismatic personality, he challenged the Jews to open their hearts to the commandments of God and bring about the realisation of his kingdom on earth. However, he not only challenged the Jews to have complete trust in God but also challenged God to liberate the Jews from their Roman oppressors and to establish His kingdom, thus bringing to fruition the promises He had made to His people. Although Yeshua was a Pharisee and most probably an accredited rabbi, his poetic inspiration lent him some of the qualities of the prophets of old.

But as Yeshua saw the early successes of his self-imposed mission, he began to consider himself as a Messiah, a privileged son of the Almighty Father, chosen to convey his message to his people and to plead with him on their behalf. If we study the development of his short ministry, we cannot fail to recognise a transformation both in style as well as in content. He began to teach in typical Pharisee language, announcing in his parables the ideas set out earlier by the school of Hillel and others, and using well-known passages from the Scriptures to make his point. But as he made an impact on the people, he became more and more absorbed in a mystical vision which stressed the supremacy of unconditional surrender to God's love and his mercy, transforming the male divinity into a maternal symbol that dispenses with the need for learning, discipline and responsibility, preferring the childhood characteristics of innocence and trust. The return to childhood innocence and nostalgic recall of the all-enveloping love between mother and child as against the father's demand for maturation and responsibility became a major theme in his oratory. With that he coupled a theme which had its roots in late Hellenistic Orphic cults and Zoroastrian Gnosticism, namely the descent of the Son of Light, the *soter* from heaven, onto the darkness of a corrupted earth, till the Pharisaic tradition is hardly recognisable.

We see this progress, or decline, from Jewish ideas to a mystery religion in the four Gospels when in the last Gospel, that of John, Gnostic mysticism is almost entirely dominant. In any interpretation of Jesus' teaching and development of his ideas we face the difficulty that what he had said was written down and made available to us almost exclusively by the Gospel writers, and we must try to differentiate what was in the writer's mind from what Jesus intended and actually said. The ideas of the Gospel writers no doubt superimposed themselves on the image of Jesus, and it is likely that they, who never met him, ascribed to him a philosophy that was foreign to him, thus transforming the Jewish rabbi, Yeshua of Nazareth, into a Gnostic saviour.

2. THE CONCEPT OF THE MESSIAH IN THE OLD TESTAMENT

In the wide spectrum of Messianic ideas, we can discern two basic forms of emphasis: in the one we see the Messiah as a political figure, and in the other as a mythological, transpolitical, spiritual figure.

The principal function of the former is 'the recovery of independence and peace for the Jewish nation, an era of peace and prosperity, of fidelity to God and his laws, of justice and fair-dealing among men, and of personal rectitude and piety. The external condition of this is liberation from foreign oppressors; the internal condition is the religious and moral reformation or regeneration of the Jewish people itself.'[2] This golden age to come represents the renaissance of the golden age of the past, the good old days of the early monarchy and revival of the kingdom under a prince of the Davidic line. Here the Messiah is a reincarnation of King David joined with the rabbinical ideals of justice and righteousness.

However, in large tracts of prophetic writings there is no mention of revival of the monarchy and no place made for the king of the golden age. Isaiah is the most important example. One could describe his prophecies as the spiritual form of Messianic fulfilment as distinct from the political type. Isaiah's vision transcends the political function of the Messiah concerned with the liberation of the Jewish nation and the punishment of its tormentors; his prophecies emphasise peace upon the whole earth and the release of mankind from the burdens of warfare. He is not only concerned with the freedom and well-being of the Jewish nation but proclaims the brotherhood of men as children of the One God: 'He shall judge between the nations, and shall decide for many people and they shall beat their swords into ploughshares, and their spears into pruning hooks; nation shall not lift up sword against nation, neither shall they learn war any more.' God's domain as the head of the human family will be acknowledged by all men, and his sons shall learn to husband the earth in peace and co-operation and not dominate her by force and fight over her against one another. The emphasis here is not so much upon the coming of the Messiah, but upon the Messianic age, the end of history and the beginning of man's fulfilment of his humanity, his maturity as desired by God. Perhaps one of the fullest expressions of the patriarchal concept of the Messianic age was given by Zechariah:

> The time will come when the Lord shall be king over all the earth; when the Lord shall be one, and his name one.
>
> *Zechariah* xiv, 9.

This is the sovereignty of heaven over earth, the universality of the true faith which embraces all men in love and justice.

However, we can discern in Isaiah an intimation of going beyond the patriarchal imagery, a reaching out towards a unification of the patriarchal and matriarchal, of the male and female principle, when God overcomes his loneliness and consummates his maleness by a marriage, a marriage that unites heaven and earth, love and justice, reason with passion:

> ... you shall be called My delight is in her, and your land Married; for the Lord delights in you, and your land shall be married. For as a young man marries a virgin, so shall your sons marry you, and as the bridegroom rejoices over the bride, so shall your God rejoice over you.
>
> *Isaiah* lxii, 4-5.

Isaiah alludes to a final reconciliation not merely between fathers and sons, but also between the male and female principles, thus releasing the world from the age-old conflict between the rival claims of patriarchy and matriarchy. The earth as the bride is to be reinstated to her full glory and mankind can rejoice in her happiness. Prophets like Daniel indeed come quite near to an affirmation of maternalistic concepts.

Thus Jewish thought encompasses the whole range of human aspirations, from primitive tribalism and its glorification of kingship and nationalism, to the dominion of the One God and his rule uniting mankind, and ultimately the resolution of male-female conflict in the visions of its greatest prophet; these visions, however, strain patriarchal man's understanding and demand an emotional readjustment of which only few are capable.

The fulfilment of his purpose, which began with the covenant between himself and the people chosen to set an example to mankind, was to come to fruition in the maturation of mankind.

69

But those who never entered the covenant, those who never knew God's purpose, had to seek a way to fulfilment by other routes without God's intellectual guidance and protection. They abandoned themselves in mystery religions that denied reason, and in apocalyptic images of world destruction. When the real world appeared to them as a fortress created and ruled over by powerful kings and tyrants who imprisoned mankind, then only the denial of reality and destruction of its edifice could release men from their bondage. The real world as well as the body becomes a prison from which the mind must escape into a heavenly realm of light that symbolises the victory of the libido, of love over rule.

Such fantasies acquire command over men's minds when their ego is weakened by a sense of helplessness and despair due to a defeat or manifest failure of their God, the divine super-ego. When the heavenly father seems to have lost his power to protect his sons and ceases to be a strong arm against their enemies, then the death wish towards him, previously repressed, rises to the surface and the sons want to kill him. His rule will all at once appear as a burden, and they want to be freed from the restraints he has imposed. The id drives, which had been held in check by the ego in obedience to the father's rule, break through and strain to take command over the minds of men. The unrestrained and uninhibited libido is symbolised by visions of heavenly forces, by a kingdom of light that sends rays down to earth to liberate mankind from the dark confines of its prison.

Psychic processes of this kind occurred in late Hellenistic cultures, giving rise to the spread of Orphic mystery cults. The crisis of the Roman occupation made many Jews susceptible to such influences, but the majority, in whom God's rule was ingrained, beseeched him to free them from their helpless position. They demanded that he overcome his weakness by breaking out of subservience to alien rule and free his people.

Many Jews and sects in Judea took recourse to the mysticism of apocalyptic writings; the notion of the end of days and of a new world to come appealed to them. A number of cults and would-be Messiahs arose and influenced the frightened, restless minds of a people in danger. Times of crisis tend to produce much self-questioning among men; a re-examination of the roots of their institutions and beliefs stimulates new enquiry and new concepts or a return to the more primitive certainties of mystery cults.

Before I go on to investigate the position of Rabbi Yeshua in this turmoil of ideas and influences which might have determined his thoughts, I want to have a quick look at the nature of Orphic cults which had spread in the region around Palestine and also in Palestine itself during the time of the Roman occupation.

3. ORPHIC MYSTERY CULTS AND GNOSTICISM

The Orphic religion had long established communities ('churches') to which anyone without distinction of race could be admitted by initiation through baptism in water. It had spread rapidly from Attica, its original home, especially to Sicily, southern Italy, Cyprus, Palestine and Syria. In these communities, wine was especially revered as a symbol of intoxication of the spirit, as an initiation to 'enthusiasm', union with the god, later called the sacrament. By this spiritual intoxication they believed that they acquired mystic knowledge with release from the bonds of reality, not obtainable by ordinary means. Above all, they abhorred prudence and orthodoxy, while they worshipped passion and the intensity of feelings, which prudence and realism, as well as orthodox religions, had denied.

There were many aspects to the Orphic religions but their foundation may be found in the ancient myth in which it was said that the goddess Rhea had forbidden Zeus to marry. At this, Zeus sought to rape his mother. (Psychoanalytically we can interpret this story as representing the incestuous wish of the mother for her son, and her jealousy of his desire for another woman.) Rhea turned into a serpent; Zeus did likewise, and as serpent with serpent, entwined into an indissoluble knot, he coupled with her. The union came to be called 'symbolon' and it continues to represent a primeval concept of cosmic oneness.

Afterwards, Zeus ravished his daughter Persephone, who had been born of this union. The child born to him by his daughter was called Dionysus. Rhea, after having been Zeus' mother, turns into Demeter, the wife-sister of Zeus and mother of Persephone, goddess of the night. Dionysus is usually depicted as a tender boy, his mother's favourite son. We can recognise in him the two aspects which Zeus also displays: on the one hand, the son and divine child protected and worshipped by the woman, and on the other hand, the father and husband, the god of man. Dionysus, however, was much more a god of women, the eternal son and darling child of the mothers. Orphic hymns tell the story of Zeus' marriage to Persephone and the birth of Orpheus from this union. According to these mystery tales, this was not a case of seduction, but was instigated by Rhea-Demeter. This shows the ancient roots of this story, its matriarchal origins, where it was still the mother who gave the daughter to a husband, and not the father who had the authority and allowed his daughters to be abducted by men of their choice. The birth of the son took place in the cave, the maternal home, and not in the house of the male; the god was born in caves, huts or stables, not in palaces or temples. Some old illustrations show the scene in the cave with the enthroned child and two Kyretes, godfathers or uncles from the maternal line, who danced around the throne with swords drawn while a kneeling woman holds a mirror to the delighted child. It is the uncle's duty to protect the child from the envious father and his brothers, the Titans.

In a subsequent story, the Titans attacked the playing child and tore him to pieces and roasted him on the fire. However, the boiled and roasted child is depicted as having large horns and this suggests that he was a sacrificial lamb. Zeus himself appeared at the sacrificial meal and with his lightning he hurled the Titans back into the underworld. We learn from the followers of Orpheus that Zeus brought law and order into the world but Dionysus brought wine and with it pleasure, love and fulfilment; he set the crown on the world's creation. But the wine is also blood and Dionysus, the symbol of love and affection, is at the same time the object of sadistic passions. The passion of love has its counterpart in the ecstasy of sadism. The oral-sadistic drives which we can observe in infants and in the unconscious of adults find here expression in mythological imagery. Dionysus not only inspired his female followers, the Bacchantes, with a passion of love, he also aroused ecstasies of sadism that overwhelmed them like a madness. In these intoxications of sadistic fury they tore him and other men to pieces, dismembering them and drinking their blood. For, no doubt, he is both the symbol of the male whom women love and also the male on whom they vent their rage, only to mourn him afterwards. Thus we see that the paragon of love is the victim of both the angry father-figures who see him as a threat to their authority, as well as of the women who discharge their long-accumulated rage against the dominant males onto the innocent and trusting young boy.

In the myths about the dismembered Dionysus – the sacrificial lamb – we see striking similarity to the Christian concept of Jesus. In the same way as Dionysus after his many trials, sufferings and adventures sits beside the throne of Zeus and shares in his power, so in the Gospels the lamb shares the

73

throne of God and receives with him the praises of the inhabitants of heaven.

Two distinct elements seemed to enter into the conception: on the one hand, the lamb is sacrificed for the redemption of man; on the other hand the lamb is the leader or shepherd of the people of God. He makes war against the enemies of God and overcomes them while the kings and great ones of the earth hide from his wrath. In Jewish apocalyptic writings, as for instance in *Enoch*, the people of God are represented as a flock and its successive leaders as sheep or rams. [3]

To return briefly to our story of Dionysus.

When he grew up, he undertook long journeys in order to spread the gift of wine so that man would drink and be intoxicated with eternal life, and marvellous adventures marked his passage through the many countries he visited. When he returned to Greece he had a soft and effeminate appearance, being dressed in a long robe in the Lydian fashion. (It is interesting to note that Lydia has long been recognised as a centre of ancient matriarchal rites.) He was received in Greece with distrust and even hostility. On his arrival in Thrace, the king of the country, Lycurgus, declared war against him and he had to flee; Lycurgus imprisoned the Bacchantes who had followed the god, and Dionysus struck the country with sterility, depriving Lycurgus of his reason. There were many other adventures in which he encountered the enmity of kings, was killed or tortured by them; but resurrected again, he defeated them and gained revenge. On the other hand, there is that part of his adventures in which he drove women mad with passion and desire, making them lose all reason and sense of reality and forget all moral responsibilities even towards their own children.

When he was thrown into prison by Pentheus, the king of Thebes, Dionysus escaped without difficulty and struck the women of Thebes with madness. They were transformed into maenads and held Dionysian orgies. Pentheus had the impudence to follow them and was torn to pieces by his own mother. (This terrible drama forms the subject of Euripides' *The Bacchae*.)

(We see here how the god intoxicated the women and released in them the passions of sexuality which were normally held in check and, at the same time, made them give vent to the rage they felt towards the restrictions imposed upon them by the male-dominated order of reality.)

Out of the suffering and resurrection of Dionysus the followers of Orphism claimed to have acquired a mystic sense in which they became one with God. In the words of Plutarch, Dionysus is the god who is destroyed, who disappears and relinquishes life and then is born again, becoming the symbol of everlasting life.

The mystic elements of Orphism entered into Greek philosophy with Pythagoras, and from Pythagoras Orphic elements entered into the philosophy of Plato, and from Plato into most of the later Hellenistic philosophies. Among the neo-Platonists, Philo, the Jewish philosopher, who was an influential member of the Jewish community of Alexandria, gave the Orphic mystery cult a prominent place in his writings. Paul was greatly influenced both by Hellenistic mystery cults as well as by Persian apocalyptic Gnosticism. The latter is based on the irreconcilable opposition between Ahura Mazda, supreme god of light, and Angra Mainyu, the evil spirit of darkness. Wilhelm Bousset has investigated the differences between Jewish and Persian apocalyptic ideas, and E. P. Sanders agrees with him that Paul's visions are much closer to the Persian than to the Jewish apocalyptic. They also concede that Jesus' apocalyptic visions were more akin to those of the Jews than the Persian form.[4]

There is no doubt that the Jews strongly resisted the Hellenistic-Orphic as well as the Persian-Gnostic influences, which were widespread at the time, just as the Egyptians forbade Orphic or Gnostic symbols in their temples. Nevertheless, there is equally no doubt that those alien images of apocalyptic religions had an impact not only on small circles of eccentric holy men but also on the Messianic hopes of many Jews.

Bousset is convinced that the paralysing anxieties which descended upon the Jewish people during the Roman occupation laid them open to eschatological expectations of a fundamental world renewal and a divine victory of God over Satan, a final judgment and many other similar fantasies that found their way into the country. He assumes that the Gospels are evidence that these religious visions were active in small circles and, moreover, were accessible to the masses, exercising a degree of influence on their belief. Bousset of course speaks from the point of view of a Christian and most probably exaggerates the impact which the apocalyptic religions had on the Jewish people. Nevertheless, it can hardly be doubted that they had a certain degree of influence; equally it cannot be doubted that the rabbis strenuously resisted it.

The question however still remains as to what extent Rabbi Yeshua came under these influences and gave them expression in his teachings or whether the Gospels imposed these foreign ideas upon him. Historical Jesus scholars tend to focus upon Jesus the Jew.

Let us very shortly try to reconstruct the probable actuality of Jesus as a Jewish young man and teacher, in order to allow us to discriminate between him and the Dionysiac figure into which he came to be transformed and made into the central object of a cult that became the foundation of Christianity.

Yeshua was born in Galilee in the village of Nazareth, the son of a carpenter by the name of Joseph, and his wife, Miriam. They had several children whom they brought up in piety and to whom they gave whatever education it was possible to give

76

at that time. Yeshua[5] ('Jesus' is the Latin form of this name) distinguished himself from the other children by his love of learning, sensitiveness and great religious devotion. As he grew older he learned his father's trade but never abandoned his studies, and continued to fill his mind with the words of the ancient prophets as well as the apocalyptic writings. Like many other Jews of his time he wondered when God would free his people from the yoke of the Romans and from their own oppressive sense of failure and guilt.

A critical moment occurred in Jesus' life the day that Johanan the Baptiser arrived at a point on the River Jordan which was but a few hours' walk from Nazareth. The pious people of the village joined those of the towns nearby and went to hear the famous preacher. Fascinated, they listened to his vivid description of the approaching Day of Judgment, and to his assurances that the Messiah would soon appear to redeem God's people and abolish all wickedness. Did they want to be saved from God's wrath? Let them repent, Johanan exclaimed. The preacher made an overwhelming impression on the sensitive spirit of Yeshua and he decided to follow Johanan's example and become a preacher.

However, the Gospels report that Johanan knew that Yeshua was the true Messiah, and he, Johanan, merely announced and prepared his coming. Can we in any way assume that Yeshua showed any signs prior to his encounter with Johanan that he was destined to become a great rabbi, a prophet or even a Messiah? It is most likely that he showed great intellectual ability, being deeply inspired by the prophets. Being a bright boy, he would ask many pertinent question of his rabbinic teachers, but such questions, far from disconcerting them or even arousing their anger as Christians imagine, would have been received with pleasure by the rabbis as a sign of talent and promise for a rabbinical career.

77

Solomon Grayzel gives a 'realistic' account of young Yeshua's development after his encounter with Johanan, and I
shall quote from it: 'Jesus had been brought up among the
poorer classes and his wandering through the country brought
him in even closer touch with the masses. He knew how hard
life was for them and he resented the superior airs which some
of the more learned assumed towards the people. Jesus emphasised for them those simple, straightforward principles which
were the foundations of Jewish teaching. He picked several of
these workmen and fishermen, and kept them as companions
wherever he went. He freely associated with others of the same
kind. He stayed at their homes and ate their bread, in complete
disregard of criticism of some rabbis that one calling himself a
teacher should act contrary to the ceremonies which the ob-
servant Jews had taken upon themselves. But his followers and
other poor people rejoiced in this championship of their cause.
Among his disciples it was agreed that Jesus must be the great
and good deliverer whose coming the Jews were expecting –
the Messiah. The leader of the disciples, Simon, who was also
known as Peter, was so sure of the fact that he mentioned it to
Jesus and was mildly rebuked.

'Jesus and his disciples decided to pay a visit to Jerusalem.
It was close to Passover, and the Holy City teemed with pilgrims
from every part of the world. Like other poor pilgrims, Jesus
and his friends camped in the open on the Mount of Olives in
the outskirts of the city. Then they went to visit the temple. A
considerable number of other Galilean Jews had heard of Jesus,
and greeting him cordially, joined his group. But no sooner did
the Galilean procession arrive at the temple than trouble began.
Jesus had looked upon the temple as God's house, the most
sacred spot in the world. He was shocked, outraged, to see
business going on within the temple grounds. He did not stop
to consider that foreign pilgrims had to change their ordinary

money into money usable for temple purposes, nor that people could not bring sacrificial animals with them. There were money-changers in the temple area; there were also stalls for animals close by. Jesus, the zealous preacher, saw in the mixture of business and religion only godlessness and sin. He turned the tables of the money-changers over and chased the cattle-dealers away. A riot broke out in the temple district for which Jesus and the Galileans had to bear the blame.

'The men responsible for public order, as well as the followers of the rabbis, saw danger in the situation. The Galileans were known to be hot-headed patriots. The Roman procurator, Pontius Pilate, was on hand with his soldiers. There was no telling what another visit by Jesus to the temple would bring. It seemed necessary to discredit him in the eyes of his followers, or to remove him from Jerusalem altogether. Some of the Pharisees felt also that Jesus was leading the Galileans away from what was considered proper Jewish custom and interpretation. In the presence of his followers, they tried to embarrass Jesus by asking him questions about the interpretation of Jewish tradition. But he answered evasively, and the discussion was without result.'[6]

Solomon Grayzel here presents a fair example of the Jewish perception of Rabbi Jesus' development, his ideas and his troubles with the authorities. It does not in any way give credence to the Gospels' description of the violent antagonism and condemnation by the rabbis. Indeed, most of his sayings gave expression to traditional Jewish concepts, as, for instance 'The Sabbath was made for man and not man for the Sabbath,' and that it was, therefore, perfectly in order for a rabbi to attend to a sick man on this day, as well as other important ethical pronouncements, as, for instance, 'Love your neighbour as you love yourself.' Such sayings as, 'It is easier for a camel to go through the eye of a needle than for a rich man to enter into the kingdom of God,' reflect the spirit of Jewish piety which deplores a man's dependence upon worldly riches and enjoins him to trust in God, and they were characteristic of Pharisaism. The opening of the 'Sermon on the Mount': 'Blessed are the poor in spirit for theirs is the kingdom,' breathes Pharisaism as well as echoing many passages in Hebrew scriptures. Hyam Maccoby maintains that some of the bitter arguments between Jesus and the Pharisees reported in the Gospels were probably amicable rabbinical discussions.

There is no doubt that Jesus was deeply moved in the presence of human suffering (*Mark* i, 43), angry with hypocrisy and the blindness of men's hearts (iv, 5), astonished at unbelief (vi, 6), indignant with stupidity and want of feeling (x, 14), and that in many of his parables he presented children as an example of trust and faith that is beloved by God.

Even references to himself as the son of God or the son of man could scarcely have aroused astonishment or enmity, for all the Jews considered themselves as sons of God, an appellation which denoted a sense of piety and closeness to God and did not in any way imply claim to divinity. His miraculous healings, which for the evangelists were ultimate proof of the divine nature of Jesus, would not be strange to Jews, for the Galilean rabbis had long developed considerable expertise in psycho-somatic medicine and the art of hypnotism. And, after all, healing the sick was a traditional function of many rabbis, who made a special study of medicine.

4. THE INFLUENCE OF ORPHISM AND GNOSTICISM UPON THE GOSPELS

However, the role of the *soter*, the divine messenger from heaven, plays a significant role in the Gospels' presentation of Jesus. Right at the beginning of Mark's Gospel, Jesus is represented as the divine Messiah who with his very presence initiates the heavenly kingdom. With him the eschatological event occurs, meaning that with the arrival of Jesus God's kingdom is established. He does not merely prepare the way for the kingdom – as this was the role of John the Baptiser – he announces its presence and the overthrow of all previous history. According to the Gospels, Jesus proclaimed the kingdom of God not as coming in the near future but as having arrived. Any Jewish teacher might have said: 'If you repent, and pledge yourself to the observances of Torah then you have taken upon yourself the kingdom of God.' But Jesus is reported as saying: 'If I, by the finger of God, cast out demons then the kingdom of God is upon you.' However, what really happened was that the spirit of Gnosticism had invaded the Gospels, transforming the rabbi from Nazareth into a supernatural figure.

Mark writes (i, 9):

In those days Jesus came from Nazareth of Galilee and was baptised by John in the Jordan. And when he came up out of the water, immediately he saw the heavens opened and the Spirit descending upon him like a dove; and a voice came from heaven, 'Thou art my beloved Son; with thee I am well pleased.' [7]

The vision of the messenger from the kingdom of light, who is to release men from the kingdom of darkness and liberate them from evil and sinfulness in an apocalyptic transformation, is even more dominant in the Gospel of John:

'I am the light of the world; he who follows me will not walk in darkness, but will have the light of life (viii, 12) ... For as the Father raises the dead and gives them life, so also the Son gives life to whom he will. The Father judges no one, but has given all judgment to the Son, that all may honour the Son, even as they honour the Father. He who does not honour the Son does not honour the Father who sent him.'

John v, 21-23.

'Truly, truly, I say to you, the hour is coming, and now is, when the dead will hear the voice of the Son of God, and those who hear will live. For as the Father has life in himself, so he has granted the Son also to have life in himself, and has given him authority to execute judgment, because he is the Son of man.'

John v, 25-27.

Jesus is not only presented in the Gospels as the incarnation of perfect righteousness, purity and truth; not only does he confer immortality upon all who believe in him, but he transcends human reason and dispenses with the rules of logic; indeed, he deliberately outrages the rabbis by contradicting their perceptions of reality and common sense. He, moreover, frequently sets out to confuse and insult them with a kind of sophistry which would hardly have convinced the learned Jews, the Pharisees, but would only have antagonised them.

When the Jews asked Jesus, 'Where is your father?' he said to them:

...'You know neither me, nor my Father; if you knew me, you would know my Father also'... 'If God were your Father, you would love me, for I proceeded and came forth from God... You are of your father the devil, and your will is to do your father's desires. He was a murderer from the beginning, and has nothing to do with the truth, because there is no truth in him. When he lies, he speaks according to his own nature, for he is a liar and the father of lies. But, because I tell the truth, you do not believe me.'

John viii, 19, 42, 44-45.

It is interesting to note that the Gospel writer knew that his Jesus was bound to make a very bad impression on the Pharisees, and he put quite reasoned arguments into their mouths;

by doing so, however, he meant to underline the limitations of reason and realism in face of the spiritual message of Jesus. The very nonsensicality of some of his sayings obviously was meant to be a declaration of war on common sense representing the bondage of earth-bound reality.

> The Jews answered him, 'Are we not right in saying that you are a Samaritan and have a demon?' Jesus answered, 'I have not a demon; but I honour my Father, and you dishonour me. ...Truly, truly, I say to you, if anyone keeps my word, he will never see death.'
>
> *John* viii, 48-49, 51.

And when the Jews objected by saying that even Abraham and the prophets had to die, and once again asked him who he claimed to be, Jesus said:

> 'Your father Abraham rejoiced that he was to see my day; he saw it and was glad.' The Jews then said to him: 'You are not yet fifty years old, and have you seen Abraham?' Jesus said to them, 'Truly, truly, I say to you, before Abraham was, I am.'
>
> *John* viii, 56-58.

This seems to have made them lose their patience and they threw stones at him; but Jesus hid himself and went out of the temple.

These reports of the conflicts between Jesus and the Jews attempt to show the Pharisees' antagonism towards Jesus, but only succeed in presenting him as making claims which were bound to affront the Jews' sense of reality or of anyone who would argue with him. It makes the Jews appear very tolerant to a preacher who had obviously taken leave of his senses and whose arguments were an insult not only to the Pharisees but to everything their religion stood for.

The image of the *soter* presented here, the life-giving messenger from heavenly regions, at the same time represents the image of a maniac who had elevated himself to the status of the omnipotent father and identified with him. When Adam ate of the Tree of Knowledge, he caused God to fear that he would eat of the Tree of Life and 'become like one of us.' And indeed Jesus has eaten of the Tree of Life and has become like God. He has accomplished what no other man before him had accomplished: he has broken the ultimate taboo. But he claims that God welcomed him and hailed him as his beloved son, and has given him divine powers and eternal life and the privilege to be a judge over men.

No Jew has ever spoken in this way, being fully aware of God's supremacy over all men. We can either assume that the Rabbi of Nazareth had become a maniac and in his narcissistic intoxication had forgotten all the fundamental concepts of his religion, or that he has been transformed by the Gospel writers into a mystic messenger of an alien religion. There can be little doubt that the second of these propositions is the true one. However, even more important than his presentation as a messenger of the heavenly kingdom, modelled on Persian Mazdaism, is the paradigm of the son of God who has to die to redeem mankind, the reintroduction of the Dionysiac cult of sacrifice of the favourite son. This concept is not only entirely alien to the Jews but considered with special abhorrence, as it flies in the face of everything that they had worked for in their spiritual development, namely, the establishment of a relationship between men and God that made human sacrifice unnecessary. Indeed, it became the central tenet of Judaism that the covenant between God and man, sealed by the act of circumcision, had finally abolished the need for human sacrifice. In fact any human sacrifice was an insult to God, for it denied the covenant.

(As we shall see, the new sacrificial cult introduced by Christianity only appealed to those who had not entered into the covenant with God; it made no sense to the circumcised Jew.)

The concept of sacrifice is introduced gradually into the Gospels. Beside the theme of manic incorporation of God's power, we find the theme of sadistic cannibalism playing an increasingly important role in Jesus' speeches, and they were particularly offensive to the Jews. In these passages he identifies with a totem animal, inviting the Jews to partake in a totem feast. He offers himself to them as the sacrificial lamb, the embodiment of love and forgiveness, and proclaims its superiority over reason and legality. He is in fact Adonis, the original messenger of love and light, who, by the radiant power of his libido, opens men's hearts to love and chases the powers of evil from earth. The beautiful youth also appears as Dionysus, the favourite son-child of the mother, eternal adversary of priests and rulers, the harbinger of liberty and the kingdom of light. But as we have seen, Dionysus is also the lamb cooked, his flesh devoured and his blood drunk in the ecstatic cults of Orpheus. In the devouring of the object and symbol of love, the worshippers partake in his libido, it floods their senses, the God is in them and his presence is forever:

'Truly, truly, I say to you, unless you eat the flesh of the Son of man and drink his blood, you have no life in you; he who eats my flesh and drinks my blood has eternal life, and I will raise him up at the last day. For my flesh is food indeed, and my blood is drink indeed. He who eats my flesh and drinks my blood abides in me, and I in him.'

John vi, 53-56.

While it appears like an invitation to cannibalism, this act is transformed into a communion with the eternal Logos – with life and light – and this transformation from sadistic destruction of the body of Christ into communion with eternal life takes place through love and faith. Those who believe will receive eternal life, his flesh and blood will be nourishment forever, and they will neither thirst nor hunger again. Those who do not believe in him will destroy him.

Jesus said:

> '...the words that I have spoken to you are spirit and life. But there are some of you that do not believe... This is why I told you that no one can come to me unless it is granted him by the Father.'

John vi, 63-64, 65.

For it is the father's love and his recognition of the son's love that makes the good incorporation possible.

> 'If any one thirst, let him come to me and drink. He who believes in me, as the scripture has said, "Out of his heart shall flow rivers of living water." '

John vii, 37-38.

He who partakes of Jesus in faith will have Jesus within him, just as Jesus has his father who loves him within him and partakes of his eternal life and omnipotence.

> 'I am the way, and the truth, and the life; no one comes to the Father, but by me... He who has seen me has seen the Father... Believe me that I am in the Father and the Father in me.'

John xiv, 6, 9, 11.

With this proclamation, the glory of Jesus as the incarnation of God is established – the full identity between father and son, the sacred union, realised. Jesus does not speak for himself as a person but for the father who dwells in him and whose purpose he merely fulfils. Jesus in his being has resolved the Oedipal conflict, and he proclaims the ultimate fulfilment of this resolution. He is completely accepted by the father, and he promises his disciples that if they accept him they will be accepted by the father as he has been accepted and become one with him. But to be fully accepted, the preoccupation with the world, the fixation upon ego drives, which are dominated by competition, rivalry, aggression and desire for power, has to be relinquished; the destructive urges which dominate in the world must be seen in their full horror and the extent of men's sinfulness exposed. Jesus has to be killed so that he can rise up to his father, and by his resurrection, the ultimate truth, and his glory, revealed to all men.

> 'Yet a little while, and the world will see me no more, but you will see me; because I live, you will live also. In that day you will know that I am in my Father, and you in me, and I in you.'
>
> *John* xiv, 19-20.

The dualism between eternal life and this world, the realm of God and the realm of the devil, is here finally proclaimed. Jesus calls upon men to give up the bondages of reality, in order to partake in eternal life and ultimate truth.

> 'Truly, truly, I say to you, unless a grain of wheat falls into the earth and dies, it remains alone... He who loves his life loses it, and he who hates his life in this world will keep it for eternal life.'
>
> *John* xii, 24-25.

We see here the final movement away from Jewish Messianic categories to categories of Orphic Gnosticism, union with God, mutual indwelling, and the transcendence from life on earth to a heavenly existence.

The Jews are shown in the Gospels to resist these invitations to relinquish the real world and follow Jesus into his other-worldly existence, and thus they are depicted as the representatives of the powers of this world, clinging to their evil ways and refusing to enter through the door of salvation. Indeed, they would refuse to give themselves up to this 'world-denial' as the Gospel writers well know, for they considered then, as they do now, that this world is not the realm of the devil but the creation of God; salvation lies in transformation of the world in the image and purpose of God, and they were called upon to set an example to mankind in its path to perfection. To deny the world would seem to them as blasphemy against God, as it is his creation and the embodiment of his will. It is perfectly true that the Jews would have objected to this part of Jesus's teaching, and no Jewish rabbi, however much he was influenced by apocalyptic writings, would have taught such a philosophy.

However, we cannot deny the appeal which the Gospels have had upon the minds of men forever drawn by infantilistic fantasies redolent with manic and sado-masochistic complexes of father-murder and expiatory sacrifices. In the ultimate teachings of the Gospel of Jesus we can recognise the trinity between the sons, the fathers on earth and the father in heaven. The father on earth represents the duties of men in reality, the obligations of gratification delay, the need to work, to strive and to struggle; it is the world of toil, ambition, competition and fear of authority. But the father in heaven is above these tribulations: he is the spirit, who lives in the realm of eternity. And his true son, who has been slain by the earthly fathers, appears to the young men, and he calls upon them to renounce their loyalty to their fathers, to leave the world of perdition and evil and come to Him.

The fathers on earth have denied the father in heaven, they do not wish to know him as they cannot face their own guilt and, therefore, they are made of lies and possessed by evil. They are men of power, they manipulate and conspire to keep it, their philosophy serves to hide the truth, and their laws are a cloak to cover up the evil within them. The sons therefore must renounce their worldly fathers and glorify the father who is in heaven so that they are freed from guilt and not stained by the sins of their fathers; and Jesus is the representative of the sons of the heavenly father who have renounced the fathers of the world. He wants them to join the father in heaven as he has done, and those who join him will not be of this world but of heaven. The fathers of this world will slay Jesus for he reminds them of their guilt, but in his death Jesus will finally reveal his immortality and the glory of everlasting life:

'Father, I desire that they also... may be with me... to behold my glory which thou hast given me in thy love for me before the foundation of the world...'
'I made known to them thy name, and I will make it known, that the love with which thou hast loved me may be in them, and I in them.'

John xvii, 24, 26.

Renunciation of the world of the earthly fathers relieves the sons from the restraints which the laws of the world have imposed upon them and they are set free. In heaven, mother and father, male and female, son and father, son and mother are finally united. In the transformations and displacements of the libido, expressed symbolically in mythological terms, the heavenly realm represents the bright pulsating realm of erotic fulfilment where restraints and limitations of this world are lifted from the minds of men and they can freely behold the realm of guiltless pleasure.

There is another important aspect to this myth. The Jews are shown as the authorities, the priests, who resist the teachings of Jesus and who are ultimately responsible for his death. They typify men who cannot bring themselves to relinquish the reign of this world and are therefore lost to salvation:

'He who loves his life loses it, and he who hates his life in this world will keep it for eternal life (*John* xii, 25)... If a man does not abide in me, he is cast forth as a branch and withers; and the branches are gathered, thrown into the fire and burned (*John* xv, 6)... As the Father has loved me, so have I loved you; abide in my love (xv, 9)... He who hates me hates my Father also' (xv, 23).

But in the same way as the Jews did not acknowledge Jesus and thus did not acknowledge the heavenly father who sent him, and persevered in their ways which are the ways of the world, so most men continue in the ways of this world and refuse to renounce it. Thus, in every Christian there is the Jew, the follower of those who are powerful and rich, the priests and the lawyers and the kings – in every man there is the evil of this world. And just as every Christian must fight against the evil which is in him in order to follow Jesus, so he must fight the Jew. He must fight the Jew in him and the Jew around him, to extinguish the internal and external manifestation of all that is sinful; the fight against the Jew is therefore a fight against the evil that is in every man.

These battles have not only tormented the soul of Christianity, they have tormented the Jews, who were, and still are, perplexed by this transformation that has come over Judaism in the name of Christianity. For Jews consider their fathers to be bound to God by the covenant and beloved by Him, and, being the sons of their fathers, are sons of the heavenly father also. In recognising their fathers as the teachers of the law and representatives of the covenant between God and man, they are constrained to keep the laws, to take to their hearts the words of the prophets and the reasoning of their rabbis.

Many Jewish scholars feel that if they could only convince the Christians that the Gospels misrepresented the Jewish religion, their paranoid fantasies concerning the Jews could be overcome and, perhaps, a new sanity based on the ethical commandments of their Torah could enter into the world. But it did not become historic reality, as mankind has not attained the level of maturity which God intended. It has clung to the archaic myths, sacrifice of the young son, the old images of Attis and Adonis, his resurrection and eternal life; it kindles the passions of Dionysiac cults; it gives satisfaction to the yearning for divine judgment that outweighs the vagaries and injustices of the judgments of lawyers and kings which have victimised people through the ages; it satisfies the craving for love that is unconditional and evokes memories of childhood enveloped in the love of mother; and it provides a satisfying sense of revenge against the fathers and all those who in their exercise of power and privilege insult and oppress the poor and innocent of this world. And what perhaps matters most of all, the Christian myth is a constant fountain-head for the emotional gratification of unconscious Oedipal drives in its dramatisation of the ultimate victory of the sons over the elders, and their entry into the kingdom of everlasting life.

But we still have not answered the question how the Gospel writers came to acquire this extraordinarily potent, at times beautiful, and, at other times, malign religion, malign because it condemned this world to be the kingdom of evil.

5. THE NAZARENES

Among the Gospel writers Matthew can still be considered a Hebrew (it is said that his name was Levi before his conversion), and his overall purpose was to show how completely Jesus fulfilled the Old Testament Scriptures, mainly addressing his message to the Jews. Indeed, we can say that while Matthew was a Hebrew, speaking to Hebrews, the three other Gospel writers addressed themselves to the Gentiles.

Mark was a disciple of Paul or, at least, was under his influence, and took Paul's teachings as the foundation for his Gospel. While Matthew wrote in Judea, Mark wrote his Gospel in

Rome in about AD 60-65, some time after he accompanied Paul on his first missionary journey.

There can be no doubt that it is Paul who provides the link between the Jewish rabbi and the Gnostic figure of Jesus as presented in the Gospels. For it was his intervention in the newly formed circle of Jesus' followers, the Nazarenes, which transformed this Jewish cult into a Hellenistic-Gnostic religion that had a wide appeal not only among many Greek-speaking Jews outside Palestine but among the Gentiles and eventually among the masses of 'second class' citizens and slaves of the Roman Empire. Paul is universally regarded as the true founder of Christianity, whose passionate faith defined Jesus' teaching and made it comprehensible to the world. For Christians he is the first who fully comprehended Jesus' system of theology, to grasp the magnitude of the changes it embodied and the completeness of the break with Judaic law. Nietzsche thought that, 'Paul embodies the very opposite type to that of Jesus, the bringer of good news: he is a genius in hatred, in the vision of hate, in the ruthless logic of hate. What has not this nefarious evangelist sacrificed to his hatred! He sacrificed first and foremost his saviour; he crucified him on *his* cross... A God who died for our sins, redemption by faith, resurrection after death, all these things are falsifications of true Christianity, for which that morbid crank must be made responsible.' There are many such views aired by Christians who are attracted to many aspects of Jesus' teachings but are repelled by Paul's sado-masochistic imagery and his obsession with sin.

But let us retrace our steps for a moment and have a look at what happened to the followers of Jesus after his crucifixion before Paul emerged on the scene, and before the Gospels were written.

The earliest followers of Jesus we know of were not called Christians, they were called Nazarenes. They believed that their great rabbi would return to life by a special miracle, that he would be resurrected by God and revealed as the Messiah. Although Jesus' disciples were mostly Galileans, the sources give pride of place to Jerusalem as the headquarters of the community. Indeed, there is some evidence that they met in the house of Mary, the mother of Mark. It is assumed that Mary was a widow and a woman of substance, and that her house was a meeting-place for the first Nazarenes in Jerusalem. It was in the 'large upper room' where the disciples foregathered after Jesus' death, and it was in this room where their rabbi celebrated his last Passover feast, better known as 'the last supper'. This group was not a separate church; it had no particular rituals, no holy places, no priests. It met for meals, had readings from Scripture; there were prayers and hymns sung, probably styled on customary Jewish tradition. They were circumcised, and would speak to each other of the inevitable coming of the Messiah, and read from apocalyptic writings that announced the end of this world, making ready for the true kingdom.

> And many of those who sleep in the dust of the earth shall awake, some to everlasting life, and some to shame and everlasting contempt. And those who are wise shall shine like the brightness of the firmament; and those who turn many to righteousness, like the stars for ever and ever.
>
> *Daniel* xii, 2-3

And they would read from Isaiah, preaching the virtue of the belief that comes from the heart and is much closer to God than all the gift-offerings and outward protestations of ritual rectitude. And they would lift their spirits with the psalms of David and the proverbs of Solomon, and they would recite the parables of their teacher Yeshua. They would most likely also debate how the message of universal salvation could be spread, and how the Gentiles could be persuaded to learn the laws and whether they would accept circumcision.

Despite their apocalyptic leanings, the earliest Nazarenes were orthodox Jews who continued to observe the law and attend the synagogue and temple. Many people must have regarded this group as a pious and humble Jewish sect, keen on charity, sharing goods and serving an unjustly treated rabbi with an apocalyptic mission. This view was shared by some priests, and a number of Pharisees became members of the sect. They were soon joined by a number of Greek converts and Greek-speaking Jews who had returned from foreign parts to live in the capital. However, it became evident that the Hellenists did not regard temple worship as a necessary part of their new-found faith, and one of them, Stephen, precipitated a crisis by a direct attack on the Jewish cultus, and on one occasion called the Jewish leaders murderers, that is to say, responsible for the crucifixion. In the ensuing quarrels the Hellenists were driven from Jerusalem.

The expulsion of the Hellenists caused a split within the Nazarene movement but at the same time laid the foundation for what was to become its most important feature, namely, the mission to the Gentiles. When one of the Hellenist Nazarenes, Philip, reached Samaria, he made a number of converts, possibly because the Samaritans, being Hellenists, rejected the temple cultus in Jerusalem. Peter and John, who came especially from Jerusalem to investigate Philip's proselytising activities, legitimised the conversions. This step of approval for Philip's activities was the first and fundamental sanction for preaching the Gospel to the Gentiles.

The orthodox Nazarenes were prepared to admit Gentiles to their community but were emphatic that they must be circumcised and obey the laws. The Gentile mission, however, became increasingly unorthodox and careless of many Jewish rules and was considered to be incompatible with mainstream Judaism. Most Jerusalem Jews, therefore, came to view the Gentile mission of the Nazarenes with misgivings.

6. PAUL: THE PROPAGANDIST OF HELLENISM

It was at this point that Paul appeared on the scene and by his teachings gave theological justification to the anti-orthodox trend in the movement. What started as a faction among the Nazarenes, who neglected many aspects of Judaic laws in order to find wider appeal among the Gentiles, was confirmed by him in a theological system which provided justification for the evangelic tendencies and, indeed, soon gave it the stamp of a new religion. He established a theology that gave systematic exposition and substance to a vision of Jesus which deliberately separated him from his Jewish roots and made him into a divine figure calculated to find universal appeal among Gentiles. He was one of the great propagandists of all time, not averse to telling lies if they increased the impact of his teaching, a propagandist of unequalled zeal, energy and relentless determination.

He presents himself as an orthodox Jew and a Pharisee, a disciple of the great Rabbi Gamaliel. At the same time it is obvious that his knowledge of the Scriptures was derived from the Septuagint, the Greek translation of the Old Testament, and his knowledge of the original Hebrew scanty. This would not be possible if he had been a student of Gamaliel, who would have expected and demanded a thorough knowledge of Hebrew and familiarity with the original version of the Scriptures. Hyam Maccoby, who made a close study of Paul's interpretation of Scripture and rabbinic literature, considers that he found incontestable evidence that Paul's knowledge was limited and typical of a Hellenist's acquaintance with Judaism. This did not prevent Paul from posing as an expert and claiming Pharisaic authority for his pronouncements. Indeed, it is no exaggeration to say that sometimes without realising it and sometimes deliberately he misrepresented Judaic philosophy in order to bring about a final separation between the Judaic and Hellenistic branches of the

Nazarene movement, to discredit the former and claim spiritual superiority for the latter. In order to understand the full extent of Pauline distortion it is worthwhile to look at the relationship of the Nazarene movement with Judaism before the destruction of Jerusalem in AD 70.

We have shown that a schism occurred among the Nazarenes, instigated by the Hellenists who intended to free the movement from its Jewish roots in order to set up a Church devoted to the conversion of Gentiles; this was resisted by the main body of the Nazarenes, who considered themselves to be orthodox Jews. But while internal dissensions and spiritual self-questioning doubtlessly played an important role in the evolution of this movement, it was not regarded as heretical by the Jewish religious authorities, the Pharisees. Indeed, the Nazarenes were regarded as forming a group *within* the Pharisees and in many respects an ultra-pious group at that.[8]

The first leader of the Nazarenes, James, the brother of Jesus, was famous for his devotion to the temple, and his meticulous observance of Jewish law. The Nazarenes observed the Sabbath and the dietary laws and, in doing so, were convinced they were following the example of Jesus. However, the movement was not only regarded as a variety of Pharisaism but also as a variety of Zealotism. Jesus was well known to be a Pharisee rebel against Rome, and his followers were therefore looked upon by the Sadducee priests and collaborators of Herodius as potential trouble-makers against Rome. They were persecuted from time to time by the priestly establishment who wanted nothing more than trouble-free co-operation with Rome. When Peter was arrested by the Sadducees he was saved by the leader of the Pharisees, Rabbi Gamaliel. When James himself, the brother of Jesus, was illegally executed by the Romans with connivance of the high priest, the Pharisees protested vigorously and succeeded in having the high priest dismissed. The self-same Rabbi

Gamaliel, whose disciple Paul claimed to be, was a vigorous defender of the Nazarene movement, but, nevertheless, Paul managed to lump high priest and Pharisees together as persecutors of the followers of Jesus.

It is well to remember that the Nazarenes played a prominent part in missionary activities in which the Pharisees were engaged at this period. The whole of the Pharisee movement was in a phase of rapid expansion and keen proselytising; but it is likely that the message of the 'good news' spread by the Nazarenes, that the Messiah had come and would soon return, was attractive to many who would have remained impervious to ordinary Pharisaism. The kingdom of Adiabene in northern Mesopotamia was converted to Pharisaic Judaism about ten years after the death of Jesus, and Roman writers testify with alarm to the spread of Judaism in the Roman Empire.

Paul, however, set about spreading the impression that the Jews, the Sadducees as well as the Pharisees, ruthlessly opposed and persecuted the followers of Jesus, to misrepresent and distort Jewish laws, and impose a Hellenistic stamp upon the Nazarenes and present them as an anti-Jewish movement. We might ask how he came to be so phenomenally successful in this propaganda and what motivated him to defame his own people by calling them the sons of the devil and 'their laws a curse upon men' (*Galatians* iii, 10).

Paul was a native of Tarsus, a town in southern Turkey with a large proportion of Hellenistic Jews. It was a centre of conflicting mystery religions, Orphic cults and Persian Gnosticism. There is little doubt that Paul was a Hellenistic Jew and that his keen and restless mind was influenced by these religious cults and teachings. While still a young man he came to Jerusalem, and *Acts* tells us that he was educated at the feet of Gamaliel, while Paul repeatedly emphasised his thorough grounding in Pharisaic Judaism. However, his interpretation of Scripture and rabbinic sayings, which ignores the Jewish emphasis on repentance and forgiveness, and his scanty knowledge of Hebrew, make it appear unlikely that he had indeed studied with Gamaliel, the great leader of the liberal school of Hillel. There are many contradictions regarding his claim to have been a persecutor of the Nazarenes. It could, however, be true that he was an agent of the high priest sent to spy among the Nazarenes.

By far the most important event which occurred in the life of the founder of Christianity was his vision on the road to Damascus, an event upon which he based his mission and his election to be the apostle of Jesus. This conversion, from being a persecutor of the followers of Jesus of Nazareth to being his apostle to the world, had a particularly dramatic effect. Whether it was true or invented by Paul is hard to decide, but we must take his claim as it stands for it is the foundation myth of Christianity. He claimed that in persecuting the Nazarenes, he was convinced

> that I ought to do many things in opposing the name of Jesus of Nazareth. And I did so in Jerusalem; I not only shut up many of the saints in prison, by authority from the chief priests, but when they were put to death I cast my vote against them. And I punished them often in all the synagogues and tried to make them blaspheme; and in raging fury against them, I persecuted them even to foreign cities.
>
> Thus I journeyed to Damascus with the authority and commission of the chief priests. At midday, I saw on the way a light from heaven, brighter than the sun, shining round me and those who journeyed with me. And when we had all fallen to the ground, I heard a voice saying to me in the Hebrew language, 'Saul, Saul, why do you persecute me? It hurts you to kick against the goads.' And I said, 'Who are you, Lord?' And the Lord said, 'I am Jesus whom you are persecuting. But rise and stand upon your feet; for I have appeared to you for this pur-

pose, to appoint you to serve and bear witness to the things in which you have seen me and to those in which I will appear to you, delivering you from the people and from the Gentiles – to whom I send you to open their eyes, that they may turn from darkness to light and from the power of Satan to God, that they may receive forgiveness of sins and a place among those who are sanctified by faith in me.'

Acts xxvi, 9-18.

I quote this passage at length for it records the traumatic event that transformed the ruthless persecutor of the followers of Jesus into their most passionate advocate and leader, eventually to become the founder of Christianity. Prior to his conversion he claimed to be a typical Jew not only obsessed with the minutiae of the law with its endless rules of ritual cleanliness, complex Sabbath laws and dietary laws; the obligation to observe the laws which he maintained, also imposed on him the duty to hunt down and exterminate those who deliberately neglected the law or denied its relevance, a heresy of which, according to him, the followers of Jesus were particularly guilty. In his self-presentation as a ruthless enemy of the Nazarenes, Paul not merely condemns himself, he presents Jewish culture and the Jewish people in an image of agonising obsessionalism that has no room for faith in God's love, for repentance and forgiveness. In doing so he completely ignores the movements which had opposed the orthodoxy of the priests and stressed the supreme virtue of understanding, love and humility, and God's tolerance for the shortcomings of men.

Now it is true that orthodoxy has a strong component of obsessionalism driven by the constant need to undo and to counteract sinful desires and to prevent them from coming into consciousness. But because they create intense guilt feelings and anxiety they have to be counteracted by obsessive rituals of purity and repetitive incantations of magic phrases, prayer

99

formulae or magic slogans to purify the mind, punctilious preoccupation with rules, and obsessive arguments designed to
prove one's righteousness. But Paul in his condemnation of
Jewish orthodoxy forgets to mention Hillel, the great advocate
of the liberal school of Judaism. Many of his commandments
had been proclaimed by Jesus as a fundamental part of his
teaching.

While Luther, many hundreds of years later, recognised the
devil as the embodiment of his own anality, Paul identified his
devilish nature with himself as a Jew; and while in his conversion he was liberated from the domain of the devil, the Jews
who rejected salvation through Jesus remained in the devil's
clutches, the incarnation of everything that is sinful, dirty and
destructive (Goethe in his *Faust* makes the devil describe himself
as the spirit who denies, who mocks all aspirations for truth,
beauty and justice).

We have here an important example of the process of splitting
and projection; the nasty, dirty and aggressive parts of the libido
are split off from the ego of the Christian and projected not
merely onto 'others' in general terms – aliens and strangers –
but onto a specific people, namely, the Jews.

There is also a splitting and projection of the Oedipus complex. While the Jews are presented as the fathers who terrorise
the sons and thwart their desire for love, they are also the sons
who have denied the heavenly father; it is Jesus and his followers
who are the true and loving sons of the father and, by rebelling
against the Jews, show their love for Him. The kingdom of the
Jews is represented as a usurpation of the heavenly father's
authority; they rule the world by betraying God. Indeed, they
are the father-killers, and the Christians are the sons who re-
instate the true authority of the father in heaven and proclaim
his glory. Thus the Oedipal sin of father-murder is split off from
the Christians and projected onto the Jews. In fighting against

Jews, Christians purify themselves from Oedipal guilt and the Jews absorb into themselves the perennial sin of mankind, they are the embodiment of the father-killers:

> And since they did not see fit to acknowledge God, God gave them up to a base mind and to improper conduct. They were filled with all manner of wickedness, evil, covetousness, malice. Full of envy, murder, strife, deceit, malignity, they are gossips, slanderers, haters of God, insolent, haughty, boastful, inventors of evil, disobedient to parents, foolish, faithless, heartless, ruthless. Though they know God's decree that those who do such things deserve to die, they not only do them but approve those who practise them.
>
> *Romans* i, 28-32.

It is, therefore, easy to understand the enormous attraction of the Christian message, of their good news which announces the liberation of mankind from its sin by having pin-pointed the real perpetrators. And the figure of the suffering Jesus, his crucifixion, dramatically represents the evil deed of the Jews. The Jews have killed both father as well as son, the loving father in heaven and his beloved son on earth.

Yet still another aspect of the deep psychological processes mobilised by Christianity is worth mentioning here: the call of the mothers, the boy's fantasies of fighting the fathers in order to liberate the goddess of his childhood from her suffering under the brutal rule of the fathers and to restore her honour and her domain. He fights for her and dies for her but in his death he gives himself up to the mother and he is also at the same time received with joy by the real all-loving father in heaven. The true God, the loving father who cherishes his wife, who in his love encompasses all human beings, loves and is proud of the son who is prepared to fight on behalf of his mother. The Cross not only symbolises the resolution of Oedipal guilt but also craving for the return to mother. Attis, the son-lover of Cybele, the mother of the gods, was driven by his mother's love for him and castrated himself upon a pine tree. Just as Attis unmans himself for the sake of his mother and has his effigy on a pine tree in memory of his deed, so Christ hangs on the Tree of Life, which is also the Tree of Martyrdom. St. Augustine actually interprets Christ's death as a sexual congress with the mother, similar to the feast of Adonis when Venus and Adonis were laid upon the bridal couch: 'Like a bridegroom Christ went forth from his chamber, he went out with a presage of his nuptials into the field of the world... He came to the marriage bed of the Cross, and there, in mounting it, he consummated his marriage. And when he perceived the sighs of the creature, he lovingly gave himself up to the torment in place of his bride... and he joined the woman (*matrona*) to himself for ever.' [9] (*Matrona* in the language of St. Augustine means the Church.) The sexual act is here transformed into its opposite – torment as pleasure. Jesus hanging on the Cross symbolises the perennial desire of man to return to mother and at the same time his submission to father. The crucifixion is thus both a sexual consummation, the Cross representing the outstretched arms of the enfolding mother, as well as submission to father. There are many references in the New Testament and Christian mystic writings to the wood of the Cross in Golgotha being made from the Tree of Life in the Garden of Eden.

Jesus, the hero, fulfils the perennial urge of mankind and he dies for it; for his bravery as the true and courageous son of man he is not only forgiven by God but exalted by him, to sit by his side in glory. In Jesus' sacrifice maternal and paternal principles are wedded and this wedding is constantly celebrated in a paean to love which embraces the universe.

But to return to Paul and take a look at the psychological forces in him that produced the fantasies and passions which were to sweep over Europe. There is considerable evidence to suggest that Paul was an epileptic, and there is no doubt that he had mystical as well as daemonic experiences. In the Second Letter to the Corinthians, he speaks of having an affliction which made him feel 'so utterly, unbearably crushed that we despaired of life itself. Why, we felt that we had received the sentence of death' (*II. Corinthians* i, 8-9).

Freud in his paper on Dostoyevsky, who was also subject to epileptic fits of an hysterical type, notes that such fits correspond to death wishes: 'You wanted to kill your father in order to be your father yourself. Now you *are* your father, but your dead father,' the regular mechanism of hysterical symptoms. And further: 'Now your father is killing *you*.' For the ego the death symptom is a satisfaction in fantasy of the masculine wish and at the same time a masochistic satisfaction. Both of them, the ego and superego, carry on the role of the father.[10] Freud's comments about such attacks are highly pertinent to the case of Paul's conversion.[11]

Paul had participated in the stoning of Stephen. That stoning had been illegal. He could have identified with Stephen, the follower of Jesus, and experienced his suffering and pain, and furthermore associated the pains inflicted on Stephen with the pains Jesus suffered on the Cross. He would have unconsciously desired that Stephen-Jesus would take his revenge upon his torturers – the Jewish authorities – and he would have felt himself to be called upon to avenge Jesus upon the Jews. Thus, the orthodox emissary of the high priest, the torturer of the Jesus people, would be visited by Jesus, overwhelmed by the bright light of his libido and elected to be his apostle to the world.

It is one of the most astonishing things about Paul's writings that they do not contain a single sentence about the life or teachings of Jesus apart from the Last Supper, his Crucifixion and his Ascension. In other words, the very core of Paul's

103

imaginings and his teachings lies in the sufferings of the beloved son at the hands of the bad fathers and his ascension to the kingdom of Love of the true father.

But the son of God who dies on the cross is also the son of man and as such symbolises the ego which has to die in order to enter through the gates of the heavenly kingdom. The ego of man, formed by attachment to the earthly father and identification with him, has to be relinquished before the soul can be saved. Those central, natural drives which relate to the real world must be renounced or destroyed so that a new spiritual self can emerge. In other words, the male ego has to be subjected to a profound masochistic experience, a castration that cuts out his preoccupation with material things and sexual urges. The identification with the tortures of Jesus is a masochistic fulfilment of the need to kill the ego which is bound to this world:

> The end of those things is death... you have died to the law through the body of Christ... But now we are discharged from the law, dead to that which held us captive.
>
> *Romans* vi, 21; vii, 4, 6.

7. THE DOGMA OF ORIGINAL SIN AND THE BATTLE BETWEEN HEAVEN AND HELL

The Early Church Fathers universalised the sinfulness of man and traced it to his very nature. Through his bondage to nature, manifest in his body and his desires, man is condemned to be sinful and belongs to an order of existence which is antagonistic to the spirit, unholy and profane. He is born in sin and is subject to the temptations of sex, greed, avarice and cruelty.

> Original Sin... is the fault and corruption of the Nature of every man that is ingendered of the offspring of Adam; whereby man

is very far gone from original righteousness, and is of his own nature inclined to evil, so that the flesh lusteth always contrary to the spirit; and therefore in every person born into this world, it deserveth God's wrath and damnation.[12]

To be sinful is the consequence of being natural; man's existence represents a battle between the kingdom of sin, i.e. his natural being, and the kingdom of heaven, which is supernatural or unnatural existence. The split between the kingdom of sin and the kingdom of heaven, between the call of nature and the call of the spirit, obliges men to purify themselves from the demands of nature, to repress their urges and to sacrifice them in the image of Christ's own sacrifice.

> The condition of Man after the fall of Adam is such that he cannot turn and prepare himself, by his own natural strength and good works, to faith, and calling upon God: Wherefore we have no power to do good works pleasant and acceptable to God, without the grace of Christ, that we may have a good will, and working with us, when we have that good will.
>
> We are accounted righteous before God, only for the merit of our Lord and Saviour Jesus Christ by Faith, and not for our own works or deservings...
>
> Christ... who truly suffered, was crucified, dead and buried, to reconcile his Father to us, and to be a sacrifice, not only for original guilt, but also for all the actual sins of men. [13]

When the Jews abolished human sacrifices, they extended the autonomy of the ego to choose between good and evil, to curb its passions and to sublimate them with the help of the divine superego. As a moral being, man is given the responsibility to choose whether God's expectations are to be fulfilled, whether God's purpose on earth is to find its realisation or whether his purpose is to come to naught. In the very last words of the Hebrew Bible it says:

Behold, I will send Elijah the prophet... and he will turn the hearts of the fathers to their children and the hearts of the children to their fathers, lest I come and smite the land with a curse.

Malachi iv, 5-6.

The punishment threatened is not due to the sin inherent in man but to his incapacity to fulfil his God-given potential, his capability of living a life of love and of understanding. This Jewish concept of human self-perfection is admirably expressed by Blake: 'Men are admitted into heaven not because they have curbed their passions or have no passions, but because they have cultivated their understanding.'

While Christianity inherited the monotheistic concept of the whole man, his mind, his body, his sexuality and his creativity conceived by the mind of God and created in his image, it transformed man into a being that was half beast and half angel, as Feuerbach has remarked. The natural half of man came to be identified with the ancient pagan symbol of sexuality – the goat – and assumed the form of the devil, whereas the divine part became denaturalised spirit, pure and untainted by man's inclinations. This split image of man, driven by two opposing forces which were considered to be in a state of war with each other, pervaded not only the imagination and thinking of the Christian Church but also its laws and its politics. The battle between heaven and hell, between God and the devil, took place not only in the individual but also in the political universe of Christianity.

This doctrine of man's fundamental sinfulness and his guilt, from which only the Church could release him, became a most powerful tool in the propaganda of Christianity and its claim to rule not only over the mind of men but also over the world. The promise of salvation became a political weapon which gave total power to kings or tyrants who managed to gain the sanction of the Church and could claim to be its representative. Secular rule would claim to be of divine origin, the king the vicar of God, and those who resisted him considered subjects of the devil and enemies of God.

Indeed, it came to pass that all law was held to be eternally valid and in some degree sacred, as the providence of God was conceived to be a universally present force which touched men's lives even in their most trifling details. Whether the king succeeded to office by election or heredity or by usurpation of power, he still ruled by the grace of God; that secular rule was of divine origin and that those who resisted it were subjects of the devil was doubted by no one. The obligations of Christians to respect constituted authority came to be deeply embedded in Christianity.

Already Paul, in his *Letter to the Romans,* wrote the pronouncement which was to be fundamental to the politics of Christianity:

Let every person be subject to the governing authorities. For there is no authority except from God, and those that exist have been instituted by God. Therefore he who resists the authorities resists what God has appointed, and those who resist will incur judgement.

For rulers are not a terror to good conduct, but to bad. Would you have no fear of him who is in authority? Then do what is good, and you will receive his approval, for he is God's servant for your good. But if you do wrong, be afraid, for he does not bear the sword in vain; he is the servant of God to execute his wrath on the wrongdoer. Therefore one must be subject, not only to avoid God's wrath but also for the sake of conscience. For the same reason you also pay taxes, for the authorities are ministers of God, attending to this very thing. Pay all of them their dues, taxes to whom taxes are due, revenue to whom revenue is due, respect to whom respect is due, honour to whom honour is due.

Romans xiii, 1-7.

For Paul, and for all important theologians after him, it was the office rather than its holder to which respect was due; the personal virtues or vices of a ruler had nothing to do with the matter. A bad ruler was a punishment for the sins of the people and must still be obeyed.

Such injunctions were to have a powerful influence on the political developments of Christian Europe. The cosmic conflict which is constantly enacted in the individual and in society is clearly expressed by St. Augustine in his book *City of God*.

Augustine (AD 354-430) was the genius of imperial Christianity, the ideologue of the Church-State alliance and fabricator of medieval mentality. Next to Paul, who supplied the basic theology, Augustine did more to shape Christianity than any other human being.[14] 'The history of the Church was for him the march of God in the world... and human life is the theatre of a cosmic struggle between the goodness of God and the evil of rebellious spirits... Man's nature is twofold: he is spirit and body and therefore at once a citizen of this world and of the Heavenly City. On the one side stands the earthly city, the society that is founded on the earthly appetites and possessive impulses of human nature; on the other stands the City of God. The first is the kingdom of Satan, beginning its history with the fall of Adam and the disobedience of the Angels and embodied in the pagan empires of Assyria and Rome. The other is the kingdom of Christ, which embodied itself first in the Hebrew nation and later in the church and the Christianised empire.'[15]

Augustine maintained that 'the powers that be in the Christian empire are ordained by God,' and that the use of force in government was made necessary by sin and was the divinely appointed remedy for sin. He regarded the appearance of the

Christian Church as the turning-point of history; it marked a new era in the struggle between the powers of good and the powers of evil. Henceforth human salvation is bound up with the interests of the Church, represented by the kings appointed by it as the vicars of God, and these interests are in consequence paramount over all other interests whatsoever.

Augustine not only gave theological justification for the establishment of the Church in society as the centre of state authority, but also provided the ideological foundation for the Christianisation of the Roman Empire. He ascribed total power to the Church as the embodiment of Christ on earth and to the rulers of nations who were appointed by the Church, and any opposition was not only futile, it was a betrayal of Christ's mission. 'Human ideas of equity were, according to him, like "dew in the desert". Human suffering, deserved or not, occurred because God was angry. "This life, for mortals, is the wrath of God. The world is a small-scale Hell." [16]

'Man must simply learn to accept suffering and injustice. There was nothing he could do about either... Augustine saw the human race as helpless children. He constantly used the image of the suckling baby. Humanity was utterly dependent on God. The race was prostrate, and there was no possibility that it might raise itself by its own merits. That was the sin of pride – Satan's sin. Mankind's posture must be that of total humility. Its only hope lay in God's grace.' [17]

Augustine thus represents the radical transformation from the human optimism of the Classical world to the despondent passivity of the Middle Ages. The mentality he expressed was to become the dominant outlook of Christianity and to encompass the whole of European society for many centuries. Christianity gave Europe some essential fragments of Jewish law, a thing which the Jews with their appeal to moral discipline would not have been able to do, but the cost of the success of Christianity was the universalisation of a split mind. By introducing the concept of original sin, Christianity intensified man's guilt about his natural self to a degree unknown in any other previous religion. Nature became evil and had to be conquered both within man and around him. But as the nature which exists in man does not cease to function, indeed, cannot cease to function, it becomes split off from the self, unacceptable to the moral ego and projected outwards where it operates as a constant enemy.

God himself became an enemy of the natural man, of man's nature, and he became ever more frightening, so that man could only relate to him through the mediation of Jesus. Without his mediation man was doomed, the inevitable victim of God's wrath. Thus, the Church, as the representative of Jesus, could present itself as the only source of man's salvation, and its claims of total power were unquestionable.

An atmosphere of fear and absolute dependency on the Church and its secular representatives dominated the Middle Ages. Never before in history had authority acquired such awe in the eyes of the people, as a constant reminder of man's sin and his innate wretchedness; it became the all-seeing eye of the superego which constantly watches the individual, seeing not only his action but his very thoughts and desires.

The Church survived when Rome had fallen, and with it survived Roman organisation. The Church inherited and took over the organisational structures of Rome and acquired a prominence without parallel. The Church alone remained as a cohesive force amid the welter of tribes and kingdoms which followed the break-up of the Roman Empire. Its bishops became the most important men in the cities, now bereft of imperial officers, and in the dioceses. Towns, for so long the centre of wealth and power, lost their pre-eminence and declined. Though they continued to exist, they were no longer the foci of power which they had been in the Roman empire. Wealth and authority shifted to the country and was bound up with landholding. The unit of society was the estate, with the lord at the head of a descending hierarchy of tenants. The tenant peasant, or serf, held his land and implements from his lord in return for rents, in labour, kind or money, and was subject to his jurisdiction. While the protection offered by the lord was often the peasant's only chance of survival in a world of famine and war, it was the Church which maintained social cohesion and unity, and it was indispensable for law and order. Moreover, from the fourth century the Church became a landed proprietor. All over the West, bishops ran large estates and provided an element of continuity between the best kind of Roman imperial estate management and the most advanced farming of the Middle Ages. In the eyes of the medieval peasant, churchmen were 'modern' farmers who kept accounts, planned ahead, invested. The Church also had a key legal instrument, the Roman-style land deed which embodied the concept of freehold. Land actually farmed by the Church grew enormously in extent; throughout Western and Central Europe the Church established itself as the largest landowner.

This development could not have taken place, or certainly it could not have endured, as Paul Johnson observes, if clerics had not proved themselves to be better-than-average farmers and land administrators. For this the development of monasticism was largely responsible, and monasteries played a key role in the development of modern agricultural estates owned by the Church. Thus the Church created a continuity between estate and state management, and it became an indispensable force in the running of the state. It held the monopoly of learning and literacy, and without clerics to help, even the simplest tasks of government – writing commands or making charters – could not be carried out. The monasteries were the only centres of organised education from the sixth century onwards and dominated intellectual life. However, it was in the interest of the Church to have strong kings to govern nations, and it gave the status of the king a new dimension of authority.

Kingship came to be regarded as a sacred office with the king more a priest than a tribal ruler. He was God's representative, and his supernatural character was symbolised in the ceremony of anointing, marking him off from other men. This transformation is most clearly epitomised in Charlemagne, an outstanding personality who in addition to being king of the Franks became at the hands of the pope the king of the Holy Roman Empire in 800. This revival of the imperial idea shows not only the medieval belief that Christendom was the heir to Rome, but also the central place that papacy occupied in Western Europe. The creation of an emperor was an attempt to give the pope a protector and partner in directing Christendom; it put imperial power under papal auspices. In government and prestige alike Charlemagne relied upon the Church. It provided the surest means for strengthening and maintaining his empire; its baptism and its bishoprics were the best guarantees of co-ordinating his own tribes into the unit of nationhood and of assimilating his enemies.

It is hardly surprising that education and Christian propaganda occupied a leading place in the Carolingian empire. Only through a literate and trained clergy could the empire endure and its objects succeed. Thus for the first time we see a conscious educational policy designed to stimulate learning. From the first, however, its end was a Christian one, and it was concerned not with reviving the philosophical speculation of Classical times but with training ecclesiastics in knowledge of the Scriptures. Its chief object was an understanding of the established truths found in the Christian Bible and in the writings of the Church Fathers. With the Carolingian empire – the Holy Roman Empire – we have the first great victory and consolidation of the Christian religion in Europe.

8. THE MIDDLE AGES: CHRISTUS VINCIT, CHRISTUS REGNAT [18]

With the crowning of Charlemagne by Pope Leo III on Christmas Day of the year 800, the papacy asserted its right to make and unmake emperors, and Christendom became the unity behind the separate Christian states. Thus the figure of Christ, the Saviour of the world, majestically enthroned at the centre of the Cross, flanked by the symbols of the evangelists and surrounded by the twelve Apostles, is an image that came to dominate the whole of the Middle Ages, conditioning the world-view of contemporaries as well as their attitude to society and public duty. The search for ultimate truth, like the search for ultimate authority, led back to a single source – the teaching and agony of Christ. It united countless tribes and kingdoms into a community of guilt, with the Church holding the key for redemption. The Cross became a symbol of magic that reminded people not only of their sinful nature but also of their salvation through Christ. It became a shield against innumerable fears and terrors, both psychological and concrete, which had beset men since time immemorial. With the political as well as spiritual victory of the Church, the dogma of man's original sin became firmly established in the consciousness of European man.

By declaring men's sexual urges to be evil, the devil's doing which had to be conquered, the Church not only gave sexual repression a new urgency, but also set in motion large-scale regression to pre-genital, infantile fantasies. Symbolic representations of archaic fantasies poured into the consciousness of medieval men and populated their universe. Devils, witches, gnomes and monsters, demons of all kinds, crowded the imagination of medieval men and found expression in their art and cosmology. A mass of facile beliefs and childish fantasies degraded the ideas of God and reduced even the concept of

Christ to primitive magic. According to Gerson, writing in the fourteenth century: 'The world is exposed to all sorts of fancies, dreams and illusions, and mysticism is brought into the streets. Many people take to it without suitable direction, indulging in too rigid fasts, too protracted vigils and too abundant tears, all of which disturbs their brains. There is a disorder of the imagination which in its turn is due to diabolical illusion.' [19]

Oral-aggressive, sado-masochistic and anal fantasies played a major role in the hysterias of the Middle Ages. 'Thus, many saints were conspicuous for their fanatical reverence for virginity, taking the form of a horror of all that relates to sex. Saint Colette is an instance of this. (She is a typical representative of what has been called by William James "the theopathic condition".) Her supersensibility is extreme. She can endure neither the light nor the heat of fire, only the light of candles. She has an immoderate horror of flies, ants and slugs, and of all dirt and stenches of all kinds. Her abomination of sexual functions inspires her with repugnance for those saints who have passed through the matrimonial state, and leads her to oppose the admission of non-virginal persons to her congregation. The Church has ever praised such a disposition, judging it to be edifying and meritorious.' [20]

Oral-aggressive characteristics found expression in the large number of demons and devils who were projected upon God and Christ. The image of the devouring Christ is vividly described by Ruysbroeck in *The Mirror of Eternal Salvation*: 'His hunger is immensely great; he consumes us entirely to the bottom, for he is a greedy glutton with a voracious hunger; he devours even the marrow of our bones... First he prepares his repast and in his love he burns up all our sins and our faults. Next when we are purified and roasted by the fire of love, he opens his mouth like a voracious being who wishes to swallow all.' [21]

114

The pious man imagined that by eating the body of Christ he entered into a holy communion with him: 'You will eat Christ, roasted by the fire, well-baked, not at all overdone or burnt. For just as the Easter lamb was properly baked and roasted between two fires of wood or of charcoal, thus was gentle Jesus on Good Friday placed on the very spit of the worthy cross and tied between the two fires of his very fearful death and passion and of the very ardent charity and love which he felt for our souls and salvation; he was, at it were, roasted and slowly baked to save us.' [22] On the other hand a nun feels quite deluged in the blood of Christ and faints. All the red and warm blood of the five wounds flowed through the mouth of blessed Henry Suso into his heart. Catherine of Siena drank from the wound in his side. It is no wonder that the medieval religion denigrated man's nature, made man ashamed of it and, at the same time, kept the degrading and painful aspects of it always in view.

At times, sado-masochistic fantasies engendered by Christianity acquired the dimension of an epidemic. We hear of flagellation breaking out in eleventh-century Italy, and then on a huge scale in the thirteenth century, after which it spread all over Europe, becoming endemic.

The flagellants marched in procession led by priests with banners and candles, and moved from town to town, parading before the parish church and lashing themselves for hours on end. The German flagellants with their rituals, hymns and uniforms were particularly ferocious; they used leather scourges with iron spikes; if a woman or priest appeared, the ritual was spoiled and had to be started again; it culminated in the reading of a 'heavenly letter', after which spectators dipped pieces of cloth in the blood and treasured them as relics. Pope Clement VI encouraged public flagellation in Avignon. Hundreds of both sexes took part. And the pillar of Spanish orthodoxy, the

Dominican anti-Semite and rabble-rouser Saint Vincent Ferrer, led a party of flagellants through Spain, France and Italy. There was orthodox flagellation, heretical flagellation and apparently secret flagellation too.

During those centuries, the Christian hostility towards the Jews emerged with especial ferocity. Sadistic fantasies of the most primitive kind were projected onto them and repeatedly culminated in violence and large-scale massacres. The ancient fantasies adumbrated by Paul and Augustine of the Jews as the sons of the devil, the Anti-Christ, the children of perdition, etc., were revived and integrated into a whole new demonology. From the First Crusade onwards, Jews were presented as children of the devil, agents employed by Satan for the express purpose of combating Christianity and harming Christians. It was in the twelfth century that they were first accused of murdering Christian children, of torturing the consecrated wafer and of poisoning the wells. But above all it was said that Jews worshipped the devil who rewarded them collectively by making them masters of black magic, so that however helpless individual Jews might seem, Jewry possessed limitless powers of evil. They were seen as the representation of all the aggressive-sadistic-destructive urges, of all kinds of perverse and filthy pursuits of which the Christian mind had been purified by the sacrifice of Jesus.

As the Christians were beset by fantasies of receiving God's blood as their food of salvation, they accused the Jews of drinking the blood of Jesus and of Christian children, and of desecrating the water, causing it to bleed. We see here a combination of sadistic fantasies split off from the Christian ego and projected onto the Jews, with a paranoic delusion which maintained that there was a world-wide conspiracy by Jews to overthrow Christendom, to murder Christian children, to profane the host and to commit other fantastic acts.

With the victory of the Christian Church and its domination

over Europe during the eleventh and twelfth centuries, the hostility towards the Jews erupted into organised persecution and mass murder. The Jew, who in the theological delusions of Christianity was seen as the persecutor and murderer of Christ, became the object of the most horrifying vengeance.

In 1285, 180 Jews were burnt to death in Munich for allegedly having bled to death a Christian child in the synagogue. In 1298, a priest was responsible for spreading the rumour that Jews were driving nails through holy wafers, thereby crucifying Christ again. Among those murdered that year, because of the fantasy of a maddened cleric, were 628 Jews in Nuremberg. (Mordecai ben Hillel, the famous scholar, was one of the victims.) In 1370, 500 Jews were dragged through the streets of Brussels and without distinction of sex or age mutilated until dead. Eighteen tableaux showing Jews driving nails through holy wafers, and blood flowing from the host, were painted in the cathedral, still to be seen.

On January 9, 1349, all the apprehended Jews of the Swiss city of Basel were burned by a mob, infuriated by Church sermons which accused the Jews of deliberately giving the current plague, known as the Black Death, to Christians. The Jewish cemetery was destroyed and the old tombstones with their Hebrew inscriptions used for building fortifications. In the German town of Erfurt, on June 26, 1221, a band of pilgrims from Friesland bound for the Holy Land stormed the Jewish quarter and killed 26 Hebrews. In the same town 3,000 Jews were murdered in August 1348, accused of poisoning the wells. The accusation was spread by Dominican monks of that city.

In 1262, in the city of London, 1,500 Jews were butchered. In 1279, 280 more were executed, and the rest driven from the city. Their possessions fell to the Crown. In 1290, King Edward I, on All Saints' Day, ordered that all Jews be shipped out of his kingdom on hired boats. Many captains drowned their

Jewish passengers for their remaining belongings. The early kings of England played a sinister game of collaboration with the bishops: the bishops got the Jews killed or exiled, the kings got their property. [23]

These are just a few examples – a minute part – of the massacres of Jews during the Middle Ages, and they continued right through the centuries from generation to generation up to our own times. 'They constitute the most abhorrent chapter in the whole bloodstained history of Christianity and are the most discreditable feature in a religion notable for the grotesque and horrifying forms of its pathology.' [24]

Another feature of the feverish imagery of the Middle Ages is worth mentioning, namely the epidemics of witch-hunts. They represent the deep ambiguity towards women endemic in Christianity. On the one hand, the woman is seen as the desexualised, pious, God-fearing, Jesus-loving, submissive and virtuous lady. She is depicted in thousands of medieval paintings and sculptures as the adoring madonna, worshipping the Jesus child or mourning his death at the foot of the cross, always with an expression of utter innocence, her eyes turned towards heaven in a gesture of faith and submission. On the other hand, she is the rampaging, sex-hungry temptress, mistress of the snake and the devil, the witch. The woman is seen in medieval imagination as a profoundly split personality, representing the split personality of Christendom.

She is either the good, sexually repressed, Christian woman or the utterly uninhibited lover of Satan, flaunting all kinds of sexual perversions and, as such it is interesting that witches began to obsess the popular imagination not long after the appearance of Mariolatry, the worship of Mary, during the thirteenth century. In the fourteenth century, epidemics of witch-hunting and large-scale trials and executions of witches took place all over Europe. Every woman became suspect of having links with the forces of darkness and of plotting against the Church. Conversely, every Christian woman was in danger of being seduced by the evil one, or of seeing him appear in her mirror. These anxious preoccupations with the possibility of their women being tempted and seduced by the devil are the consequence of the repressed male's fear of sexuality. While the libido is split off from the ego of the good Christian and projected onto the devil, the woman would be attracted to him (the devil) and he would play a lively and dangerous role in her erotic fantasies; she would rebel against the God who denies her natural instincts and ally herself to his enemy.

The ancient images of the angry goddess who rebels against the male re-emerged in the mind of medieval man.[25] She would be a major threat to the bond between father and son, from which she is excluded, and she would seek vengeance against them and the civilisation which upholds man's love for his God as the supreme virtue. In her fury she threatens to bring 'a sterile blight upon the earth and pock its surface with infections.'

The medieval vision of the universe represents man's precarious balance between the underworld, which is a morass populated by dragons, snakes, toads, spiders, witches and devils stoking the fires of hell where the souls of men are heard to scream in anguish, and the world above, where everything is bright, calm, peaceful and harmonious, where love reigns and no evil is ever thought. The earth and all human existence is seen to be in a state of suspension between two eternal realms, and the demons and devils of the underworld constantly clamour to take possession of the minds and bodies of men and can only be warded off by Christ on the cross, the symbol and weapon of the heavenly powers. The images created by theologians, poets and painters represent the cognate universe, they are the cosmology of the time. The Holy Trinity of theology has its existential representation in the trinity of heaven, earth and hell.

Earthly existence thus has no autonomous or independent existence but is essentially a temporary battleground of two cosmic powers – heaven and hell – the state of beatitude and the state of sin.

A sombre melancholy weighed upon people's souls: whether we read a chronicle, a poem, a sermon, a legal document even, the same impression of man's sadness is produced by them all. In the literature of the time, and above all in painting, we see an image of man which we would now describe as strangulated by an overwhelming sense of guilt; this state, however, also evokes profound yearnings for release from the sin that holds people in bondage, a release into a world of light, of sweet reconciliation and forgiveness. The bitter-sweet melancholia of *dulcedo Dei* was considered by Huizinga to have been one of the most active elements of religious life of the Middle Ages. We can surely diagnose this melancholy as a mourning for a state of perfection which a loving God had intended for man, but which men were unable to achieve. Prayers for forgiveness and for divine compassion with human frailty outweighed by far the determination to study God's laws and uphold man's responsibility for living in accordance with them. A deep sense of having failed God, of having disappointed him pervaded the consciousness of the time and aroused a feeling of God's anguish over the incapability of his children to fulfil the tasks he had given them. Having lost contact with the purpose which God had in mind for them, men became helpless playthings of evil forces, utterly dependent upon divine intervention and grace. Man had lost the image of the human being that unites in himself both the divine spirit and the forces of nature and encompasses the manifold of desires and aspirations into an overriding purpose of life.

The fourteenth century was ruled by a preoccupation with death. Villon and his contemporaries were obsessed with it.

Because so many men's thoughts were set on death, the doctrine of purgatory and the possibility of buying indulgences to shorten its duration gained a new importance at a time when wars made the old way of saving one's soul by repentance and pilgrimage impossible; and such abuses profoundly undermined the faith. England and France wore themselves out in the Hundred Years War (1339-1453), and the Wars of the Roses (1455-85); the employment of mercenaries changed the basis of feudalism. Everywhere, but especially in France and England, plague, pestilence and famine followed and accompanied war. There was a decadence, and out of that decadence arose a new civilisation. The spirit of humanity was reborn and the Renaissance spread from Italy to the Western world, giving a new optimism and confidence in the future.

But in the East the medieval pathologies of Christianity continued and developed with relentless ferocity in the religion of Islam.

Notes to Christianity.

[1] John H. Hayes and J. Maxwell Miller (Eds.): *Israelite and Judean History*, SCM Press – O.T. Library, 1977, p. 641.

[2] George Foot Moore: *Judaism in the First Centuries of the Christian Era*, Vol. 2, Cambridge, MA, 1958, p. 324.

[3] C. H. Dodd: *The Interpretation of the Fourth Gospel*, Cambridge University Press, 1970, p. 231.

[4] E. P. Sanders: *Paul and Palestinian Judaism*, SCM Press, 1977, pp. 8, 33, 214, 552-6; Wilhelm Bousset: *Die Religion des Judentums im späthellenistischen Zeitalter*, Mohr, 1966, Chapter 25.

[5] Jewish scholars consider 'Jeshu' or Joshua the correct rendering of this name.

[6] Solomon Grayzel: *A History of the Jews*, Mentor, New American Library, 1968, pp. 132-133.

[7] This is a fairly straightforward expression of Orphic initiation rites.

[8] Hyam Maccoby: *Revolution in Judaea,* Orbach & Chambers, 1973, p. 232, and *The Mythmaker: Paul and the Invention of Christianity*, Weidenfeld & Nicolson, 1986, p. 51.

[9] St. Augustine: *Sermo suppositus*, 120. 8. Quoted in C. G. Jung, *Mysterium coniunctionis*, CW 14, p. 32, note 176.

[10] Sigmund Freud [1928b]: 'Dostoyevsky and Parricide', Standard Edition XXI, 185.

[11] C. R. Badcock: *The Psychoanalysis of Culture*, Basil Blackwell, Oxford, 1980, pp. 158-159, 161.

[12] *The Book of Common Prayer*, Articles of Religion, ix.

[13] *The Book of Common Prayer*, Articles of Religion, x, xi, ii.

[14] Paul Johnson: *The History of Christianity*, Penguin, 1978, p. 112 and p. 121.

[15] George Sabine: *A History of Political Theory*, Harrap, 1937, p. 191, and pp.189-190.

[16] *See* Paul Johnson: *The History of Christianity*, pp.121-122.

[17] *Ibid.*

[18] The last verse of the *Laudes* or liturgical acclamation with which a new emperor was consecrated.

[19] J. Huizinga: *The Waning of the Middle Ages*, Pelican, 1972, p. 186.

[20] *Ibid.* p. 187.

[21] *Ibid.* p. 191.
[22] *Ibid.* p. 191.
[23] Dagobert Runes: *The War Against the Jew*, New York, Philosophical Library, 1968, pp. 21, 67-68, 115.
[24] Christopher R. Badcock: *The Psychoanalysis of Culture*, p. 233.
[25] *See* George Frankl: *The Social History of the Unconscious*, Open Gate Press, London, 2003, pp. 115-123.

PART 3 Islam

Islam

FOREWORD

I have rarely experienced such resistance to writing a piece as I do now in the third part of my trilogy on monotheism. On asking myself the reason for my unwillingness to enter into the task of explaining the nature of Islam, I realise that I am not in sympathy with its extreme and all too often violent hostility towards cultures and nations which do not agree with its fundamental beliefs. The frequent declarations of Islamic leaders and clerics calling for the death and destruction of infidels provoke not only utter astonishment but horror among the intended victims of Islamic fanaticism.

How is one to react to people who declare that 'You, the infidel, love life, and we love death' or 'If you don't stop your injustices and are not prepared to submit to Allah's commandments, raw blood will flow and the attacks against you up to now are small compared with what is in store for you. You will lose life but we shall be rewarded with the pleasures of paradise'?

One is inclined to think that people who make such pronouncements with utter conviction and as a fundamental statement of religious belief must be mentally deranged – and we shall probably not be wrong to arrive at such a conclusion – but they have the full agreement and support of Islamic officialdom.

In the most sacred mosque of Islam, Sheikh Abd al-Rahman al-Sudais of the Grand Mosque in Mecca uses his sermons to call for Jews to be 'annihilated' and to urge the overthrow of Western civilisation. 'The most noble civilisation ever known to mankind is our Islamic civilisation... Only one nation is capable of resuscitating global civilisation, and that is the nation [of Islam].'

Al-Sudais is the highest imam appointed by the Saudi government, and his sermons are widely listened to across the Middle East.

Saudi Arabia, whose flag shows a sword, seems unabashed about its desire for Islam to take over the world. Its Islamic Affairs Department makes it clear that the Muslims are required to raise the banner of *jihad* in order to make the Word of Allah supreme in this world.

Saudi Arabia's education ministry encourages schoolchildren to despise Christianity and Judaism. A new schoolbook in the kingdom's curriculum tells six-year-olds: 'All religions other than Islam are false.' A note for teachers says they should 'ensure to explain' this point. In Egypt, the schoolbook *Studies in Theology: Traditions and Morals* explains that a particularly 'noble' bit of the Koran is 'encouraging the faithful to perform *jihad* in God's cause, to behead the infidels, take them prisoner and break their power.'[1]

If one engages in an investigation of natural or cultural phenomena one must have some interest and empathy with the things one intends to study. Certainly one needs a certain familiarity with them, but I find that I am not familiar, nor have any sympathy, with a religion, and its commandments, which violates my belief in the respect for life and tolerance for those who do not share my own religious convictions. I am familiar with Western religions and the traditions of the Enlightenment, with Greek and Renaissance philosophy proclaiming the freedom of speech and discussion, of reflection upon the merits of one's own beliefs. How can one feel a degree of empathy with those Islamic preachers who, by their intense study of the Qur'an, claim to have understood the teachings of Muhammad,

128

preach Holy War against the infidels of the West and the Jews and the sacred duty of true believers to kill as many people as possible – women, children and innocent bystanders – and command young people to be suicide bombers in the service of Allah in order to enter heaven as holy martyrs and enjoy the pleasures of seventy virgins? One can only feel outraged and find it unbelievable that such individuals can preach such atrocities as the highest virtue of their religion.

But curiosity, 'holy curiosity', as Einstein called it, overcame my resistance, and I wanted to find out why a pathology, which in many respects one can consider a collective psychosis, has come to dominate a religion which now has more than a thousand million followers and is threatening to introduce an age of terror, not only in the West but across the world in its determination to make humanity submit to its power. How did it come about that a religion which proclaims the belief in the one universal God who has created all life and is particularly proud of his supreme creation, namely mankind, and declares all human beings brothers and sisters under His paternity, has come to preach hatred of fellow humans who do not submit to its particular vision of God? It not only demeans the glory of humanity as the children of God but betrays God's purpose. Or so it appears.

Muslims not only consider themselves to be the children of God but also the descendants of Abraham and claim to be the true followers of the Bible. Indeed, they consider Abraham to be the founder of the Islamic religion.

I want here to remind people of the extraordinary prophecy told in the Bible some 1,200 years before Islam was created by Muhammad. Abraham, as we have seen, lived 1800 BC, while Muhammad was born about AD 570. If we allow that *Genesis* was actually written about 500 BC, it is still about 1100-1200 years before Muhammad heard Allah's voice speaking to him in AD 611. I shall quote from *Genesis* xvi onwards, where the origins and the destiny of the Arab peoples were foretold.

1. GENESIS: THE ORIGIN AND DESTINY OF MUSLIMS

Now Sarah, Abraham's wife, bore him no children. She had an Egyptian maid whose name was Hagar; and Sarah said to Abraham, 'Behold now, the Lord has prevented me from bearing children; go in to my maid; it may be that I shall obtain children by her'... And he went in to Hagar, and she conceived; and when she saw that she had conceived, she looked with contempt on her mistress. And Sarah said to Abraham, 'May the wrong done to me be on you! I gave my maid to your embrace, and... she looked on me with contempt'... But Abraham said to Sarah, 'Behold, your maid is in your power; do to her as you please.'[2] ...So she said to Abraham: 'Cast out this slave woman with her son'... And this was very displeasing to Abraham on account of Ishmael his son. But God said to Abraham, 'Be not displeased because of the lad and your slave woman; whatever Sarah says to you, do as she tells you... and I will make a nation of the son of the slave woman, because he is your offspring.' So Abraham rose early in the morning, and took bread and a skin of water, and gave it to Hagar, putting it on her shoulder, along with the child, and sent her away. And she departed and wandered in the wilderness of Beersheba.[3]

...And as she sat [with the boy], the child lifted up his voice and wept. And God heard the voice of the lad; and the angel [sent by God] called to Hagar...'What troubles you, Hagar? Fear not; for God has heard the voice of the lad... Arise, lift up the lad, your son, and hold him fast with your hand [and make him drink], for I will make him a great nation.'[4]

And God was with Ishmael, and he grew up; he lived in the wilderness, and became an expert with the bow... and was circumcised when he was thirteen.[5] And God said [to Abraham,] 'As for Ishmael... I will make him fruitful and multiply him exceedingly; he shall be the father of twelve princes, and I will make him a great nation.[6] ...As for Sarah your wife... I will bless her, and moreover I will give you a son by her.' ...Then Abraham fell on his face and laughed, and said to himself, 'Shall a child be born to a man who is a hundred years old? Shall Sarah, who is ninety years old, bear a child?' And Abraham said to God, 'O that Ishmael might live in thy sight!' God said, 'No, but Sarah, your wife, shall bear you a son, and you shall call his name Isaac. I will establish my covenant with him as an everlasting covenant for his descendants after him. As for Ishmael, I have heard you; I will bless him... But I will establish my covenant with Isaac, whom Sarah shall bear you at this season next year.'[7]

...And Sarah was listening and heard what God said. Now Abraham and Sarah were old, advanced in age; it had ceased to be with Sarah after the manner of women. So Sarah laughed to herself, saying, 'After I have grown old, and my husband is old, shall I have pleasure?'... And God said, 'Is anything too hard for the Lord? At the appointed time I will return to you, in the spring, and Sarah shall have a son.'[8]

The Lord visited Sarah... and the Lord did to Sarah as he had promised. And Sarah conceived, and bore Abraham a son in his old age at the time of which God had spoken to him... And Abraham called him Isaac. And Abraham circumcised his son Isaac when he was eight days old, as God had commanded.[9]

I have quoted at length from the rather circuitous narration in *Genesis* xvi – xxi.

We must ask why the Bible writers went to great lengths to describe the circumstances and complexities of the birth of Ishmael and Isaac, the former to be cast out with his mother into the desert where he is with God's blessing to become the father of a great nation accomplished in weapons of war, and have many princes, leaders and warriors among his descendants. They will be the bedouin of the desert, seeking for fertile oases to conquer, and conquests will be a blessing to them.

Even up to the present time victory in wars and conquests is a sign to them from God that he approves, and supports them. But what does the rivalry between Sarah and Hagar mean to teach us?

While God blesses Ishmael and promises to look after him, he makes an eternal covenant with Isaac and his descendants. And Sarah will be the mother of a great nation blessed by God, and all the people of the nations will be blessed by God. The writers of this part of *Genesis* obviously wanted to make sure that the descendants of Abraham are at the same time the descendants of the woman who loves Abraham, and he loves Sarah, and that in their love for each other they fulfil God's intention. It is through God's love for them that their sexual union is blessed by God and their descendants inherit God's blessing and his love. The mother of nations receives God's blessing together with her husband; male and female are united in the act of procreation and their offspring blessed by this union. Hagar was not Abraham's wife, nor did he love her; the spirit of God's love did not unite them, and while Ishmael was protected by God he was not chosen by Him; His spirit had not entered him.

The spirit of love did not enter into him, and God did not make a covenant with him, even though God promised that Ishmael would be the father of a great nation but not the spiritual inheritor of God's design. The woman who loved her husband and was loved by him was chosen by God to perpetuate the spirit of the universal creator who loved humanity and intended that his love for his supreme creation would unite them in their love for life. Thus man and woman, father and mother, are one in the life of humanity. There would be no rivalry between mother and father, between matriarchy and patriarchy, but in their communion they would create a community of mankind. There is to be no feeling of sin in sexuality, but the pleasure would be a joy sanctified by love, and they would be equal in the family and in the nation. But if the love between them is denied or absent then pleasure becomes a sin and contradicts God's intention and produces discontent, and anger would enter into their souls. Father and mother would be disunited and their children afraid; and when they grow up they will want to attack the world for having denied them their love and their pride and made them feel outcasts.

We must ask why the descendants of Ishmael came to worship a God who commands them to wage war with nations and religions that do not submit to him. How did this God become an angry God, and also why did he order that women should lose their power as mothers of the nation and that they were to hide themselves before men and deny their innate desire for love and sexual pleasure and men's desire for them? Why do they have to cover their bodies and their faces and make themselves invisible? Why do they have to hide their personalities, and indeed are harshly punished if they walk in the street unaccompanied by their male protectors, brothers, fathers or husbands? And why are they not allowed to speak to strangers but are kept under strict control by the males in their families and are subjected to punishment whenever they are seen to transgress these rules and displease their male relations; and, indeed, why does God expect the husband to beat his wife whenever she does not follow his orders? Why are they forbidden to enter the mosque and participate in the rituals of prayer five times a day to show their complete submission to Allah? Why do the males expect to be forgiven for their sins, while women's sins are irredeemable? What is the eternal sinfulness of Muslim women?

We may trace this belief of women's fundamental sin, which makes them hide not only their sexual desire but also their personality, to a trauma in primeval time, their cultural infancy. Not having received God's blessing as the descendants of Hagar, their seductiveness has to be hidden and their very nature denied.

But in order to be fruitful and multiply to create a great nation, men had to engage with women in the act of procreation. But the hearts of men were filled with anger for not being allowed to seek the pleasure of their woman, the pleasures of the body and the appreciation of her personality. They would give vent to their frustration by engaging in wars and conquering those who had the privilege of wealth and the love of woman which had been denied to them. The nomads of the desert of the Arabian peninsula glorified in wars against those whom they felt to be the privileged nations beyond the desert. By the dreams of conquests they would rehabilitate their pride, and they needed a God who sanctified wars.

Peace would have meant acquiescence to a world of injustice; war was a liberation from the injustices they have had to suffer. And there came to be many opportunities for warfare between tribes and nations.

2. THE BREAK-UP OF THE ROMAN EMPIRE, THE COUNCIL OF NICAEA, AND THE SEARCH FOR THE ONE GOD.

Three centuries after the crucifixion of Christ, a growing religious turmoil was gripping Rome. His followers had multiplied exponentially, and Christians and pagans began to fight each other and threatened to tear Rome apart.

The emperor Constantine decided that something had to be done. In AD 325 he resolved to unify Rome under a single religion, namely Christianity. He could see that Christianity was on the rise, and he resolved to convert his Sun-worshipping pagans to Christianity. While the followers of Jesus honoured the Jewish Sabbath on Saturday, one of Constantine's first steps in this direction was to shift it, to coincide with the pagan veneration of the Sun, to Sunday.

The affirmation of Jesus as the Son of God was officially proposed and voted on at the Council of Nicaea. By endorsing Jesus as the Son of God, Constantine turned Jesus into a deity who existed beyond the scope of the human world, an entity whose power was unchallengeable. This he thought would not only preclude further pagan challenges to Christianity but also enable the followers of Christ to redeem themselves *only* via the established sacred channels – the Roman Catholic Church.[10]

Thus the empire had become legally and theologically Christian, and it was hoped this would put an end to the turmoil and bitter rivalries within the empire. After endless debates and recriminations, the Council of Nicaea in AD 325 called upon Eusebius of Caesarea, whose learning was greatly respected, to propose a creed:

> We believe in One God, the Father Almighty, the Maker of all things visible and invisible. And in One Lord Jesus Christ, the Word of God, God from God, Light from Light, Life from Life, only-begotten Son... before all the ages, by Whom also all things were made, Who for our salvation was made flesh and lived amongst men, and suffered, and rose again on the third day, and ascended to the Father, and will come again in glory...

After many arguments Constantine dropped his bombshell on the Council: the relationship of the Son to the Father might be expressed by the word *homoousios* – 'of one essence'. It meant that the Son had no resemblance to created things, but was like the Father alone, and was of no other substance but of the Father, of the same substance as God the Father. Thus he was unlike any human being, not created by the Father but of the Father: he was God. Jesus the son had no resemblance to created things. And being God he was omnipotent, his powers were without limit, and the Roman Empire was to be the embodiment of his universal power.

For Constantine the creed was intended to be the instrument whereby unity was to be achieved among the various warring factions of the empire. The adherents of the Nicene Creed were to teach all nations, baptising them in the name of the Father, the Son and the Holy Ghost.

Constantine himself communicated to the Churches the Council's decision. His letter is notable for its strongly anti-Semitic flavour: 'It seems unworthy,' he writes, 'to calculate this most holy feast according to the custom of the Jews, who, having stained their hands with lawless crime, are naturally, in their foulness, blind in soul... What right opinions can they have, who, after the murder of the Lord, went out of their minds and are led, not by reason, but by uncontrolled passion?' The main object of Christianity is to sever 'all communication with the perjury of the Jews.'

The day on which a Roman emperor was converted to Christianity proved an unfortunate one for the Jewish people. From henceforth the contemptuous toleration which the Roman government had hitherto shown towards Judaism changed slowly but steadily into hostility, culminating in the drastic penal laws of the most orthodox emperor, Justinian. The convictions of the early Jewish followers of Jesus were totally superseded by the new Christian orthodoxy and were now heretical.[11]

But the turmoil within in the empire did not cease. Indeed, after Constantine's creed had been formally imposed upon the Council of Nicaea the conflicts between the various sects re-emerged and if anything became more vindictive in the struggle for power over the different interpretations of the true nature of Christ and for political control.

Christianity was for Constantine pre-eminently a true belief and a divine law by which to judge the bishops and the people who followed them, and their governments. Their local representatives and councillors gradually were no longer guided by conviction but by motives of self-promotion; the spiritual and moral beliefs inevitably waned in the Church.

The old corruption and oppression of the masses by officials and landlords went on unabated, and the last remnants of public spirit faded away.[12] To contemporary Christians the things of this world were of little moment, and the best Christian hesitated to touch the problems of public life, lest he be defiled. The object of the Church was not to reform the empire but to save souls. Men of high conviction became bishops, defending their own versions of the Christian creed, and government was left in the main to careerists.

Nevertheless, the future of Christianity was secured with its official adoption by the Empire, for Christianity had acquired the prestige and glamour of the Roman name: Roman Catholicism.

When Constantine built a large palace and churches in the city that came to be called Constantinople, it replaced Rome as the capital city. It is a paradox of his life that the more determined Constantine and his followers were to consolidate the Roman Catholic rule after the Nicene Council, the more the conflict between his followers and the believers in the earlier form of Christianity came to the surface and created fierce controversies regarding its true nature. It was a time of confusion and insecurity. The certainty of belief had been undermined and people were looking for the true and eternal God.

To the east of the Roman Empire lay the empire of the Sasanians, whose rule extended over modern Iran and Iraq, containing regions of high culture and ancient cities. The different ethnic groups were divided from each other by steppes or deserts, preventing easy contact between them. From time to time they were united by strong and lasting dynasties, such as the Sasanian, whose original power lay among the Persian speaking peoples of southern Iran. They were a centralised government, and ruled through a hierarchy of officials. They tried to provide a solid basis of unity by reviving Zoroastrianism, the ancient religion of the area. Under the Sasanians, Zoroastrianism was established as the official state religion, with its own priestly hierarchy. They supported the power of the ruler, who was regarded as a just king, preserving harmony between the different social groups.

The Sasanian capital, Ctesiphon, was in the fertile, populous area of central Iraq. As well as the Zoroastrians, there were Nestorian Christians, and the area was a centre of Jewish religious learning. There were also Manichaeists, and the region was a refuge for pagan philosophers and medical scientists from the Greek world. Various forms of the Persian language were spoken, and Aramaic was widespread throughout the Middle East.

But to the south of these empires, the greater part of the Arabian peninsula was steppe or desert, with isolated oases. Here the inhabitants spoke dialects of Arabic and many were nomads. Some were settled cultivators in the oases, or traders and craftsmen in small towns.

There was a precarious balance between the nomads and settlers. The camel-nomads, mobile and armed, together with the merchants of the towns, dominated the cultivators and craftsmen. The nomads were not controlled by a stable coercive power, but were led by chiefs, belonging to local families. These gathered more or less lasting groups of supporters, who expressed their cohesion and loyalty in the tribal idiom of common ancestry. They worshipped gods who dwelt in a *haram* or sanctuary, in a place or town set apart from tribal conflict and under the protection of a neighbouring tribe. The *haram* was a centre for pilgrimage, sacrifice, meetings and arbitration.

The people of the desert retained their ancient way of life, even while they increasingly came into contact with the turmoil which had befallen the great empires. Their poetry was a register of the events of their lives, or the expression of a collectively shared memory. The mood of the poetry, called the *diwan* of the Arabs, was not erotic so much as a commemoration of the transience of human life:

> The abodes are deserted, the places where we halted and those where we camped... are abandoned. In the flood-courses of Rayyan the riverbeds are naked and worn smooth, as writing is preserved on stone. The blackened dung lies undisturbed since those who stayed there are departed; long years have passed over it, years of holy and ordinary months. [13]

The way of life among the people of the Arab peninsula was the product of life in the desert – a constant looking for oases with their life-giving water and areas of fertile land around them. And the only way they would have access to them was by conquest and the employment of their craftsmen and farmers for the cultivation of the fertile land. While they depended upon the natives of the oases, they did not generally mingle with them, nor did they adopt their religions and myths. The bedouins of the desert occasionally became administrators and rulers of the conquered territories, but kept their ancient tribal loyalties.

Throughout the sixth and seventh centuries AD, the Near Eastern world was in turmoil. The Byzantine and Sasanian empires engaged in many wars between AD 540 and AD 629. The questions and doubts about the meaning of life and the way it should be lived, began to affect the way of life of the tribal nomads.

The religion of the nomads had no clear traits. Their gods, identified with objects in the sky, were believed to reside in stones, trees and other natural objects; good and evil spirits were thought to roam the world in the shape of animals; magicians and soothsayers claimed to speak with supernatural wisdom.

It was a world of animism, where the spirit which dwelled in animals and other manifestations of nature would speak through the tongues of shamans, or magicians and priests. But their images were local, and interpreted by the people according to custom and family-based tradition.

But in their encounters with the world outside, they realised that their own beliefs did not have the sense of universality and authority of the great religions and empires. And they began to feel insecure. Even their ancient ethos of conquest and loyalty to common ancestry seemed inadequate compared to the authority of a God who governs the universe and the affairs of men. When they became acquainted with the God of the Jews and his messenger Abraham, whom He called upon to be the founder and father of a new religion, the Arabs wanted to be part of Abraham's divinely ordained message, and claimed God's authority for the foundation of a new Arab nation which would unite the world in the kingdom of God. Their ancient virtues of conquest and their powers in warfare would receive the sanction and assurance of God's universal and eternal power and wisdom. The world would no longer be subjected to the fallibility of human minds, their rulers, their tribes and nations, but by unquestioning submission to God's Will, His wisdom and purpose. Those who believed in Him would be blessed and would unite the world under His rule. And after many centuries the Arab bedouins will become the leaders of God's kingdom and the teachers of His commandments.

It is not quite clear how the bedouins of the desert became acquainted with the Bible and in particular with *Genesis* and Abraham's divine mission, but they had plenty of opportunity to hear and read about it. The traders of the city would have got to know many Jews as well as Christians who by the early seventh century AD had settled in towns.

There was a world waiting for a guide, a divine authority, and for a man searching for a vocation; there was a seeker after God who expressed his wish to be taught:

'O God, if I knew how you wished to be worshipped, I would so worship you, but I do not know.'

Jewish rabbis, Christian monks and Arab soothsayers predicted the coming of a prophet, and it was to be Muhammad.

A monk, who met Muhammad on a trading journey to southern Syria, 'looked at his back and saw the seal of prophethood between his shoulders.' Natural objects saluted him: 'Not a stone or tree that he passed but would say, "Peace unto you, O apostle of God!"'

It seems that a yearning for a divine message emerged and filled many people with a hope for a new world, a reawakening of the visions of a divine revelation.

Muhammad became a solitary wanderer, expecting some heavenly message to come to him. And then, one day, perhaps when he was forty years old, something happened: some contact with the supernatural, known to later generations as the Night of Power or Destiny. In one version, an angel, seen in the form of a man, called to him to become a messenger of God.[14]

One cannot avoid comparing Muhammad's revelations to Paul's vision of Jesus, who instructed him to be his spokesman and spread his message to the world. However, Paul spoke in some detail of the background which led him to become an apostle of Jesus, the son of God, resurrected from death on the cross – from being the persecutor of Jesus' disciples whilst in the service of the High Priest, to becoming his servant, proclaiming his divinity and laying the foundations of Christendom. What do these two men have in common? What were

141

their backgrounds which made them founders of new religions which were destined to become major powers in the world? There was, and still is, much speculation about and research on the state of mind, the psychological motives of Paul's conversion and vision, but as far as I have been able to find out, nothing is known about Muhammad's psychological condition that led him to hear the voice of God and instructed him to proclaim his message.

Max Brod, among others, considered Paul to suffer from epilepsy, a condition which sometimes produces hallucinations of a supernatural power, and many psychoanalysts, including Freud, made a thorough investigation of the indications that Paul had suffered from it. Paul himself complained of periods of mental stress which disturbed and frightened him. We know nothing about this as regards Muhammad.

It has been reported that the vision of the supernatural visited many others in the Arab world at that time, but those who responded wholeheartedly and without reservation were few. Among them, however, was Muhammad's wife Khadija who steadfastly supported and encouraged him in his vision:

> Rejoice, O son of my uncle, and be of good heart. By Him in whose hand is Khadija's soul, I hope that thou wilt be the prophet of His people.

The call for a universal and all-powerful God was widespread among the Arabs of that time; when they encountered cultures which worshipped a God, the founder and begetter of the universe, the father of mankind, they felt alone, outcast, depressed and that their life was meaningless, without purpose and without guidance.

Muhammad was born about the year AD 570 in Mecca. His father died before he was born, and his mother Aminah died when he was still a small child, perhaps five or six years old,

142

so that he was brought up at first by his grandfather and then by his uncle Abu Talib. As a youth he travelled with the trading caravans from Mecca to Syria, and at the age of twenty-five married Khadija, a rich widow, fifteen years his senior. Meanwhile he had acquired a reputation for honesty and wisdom, and had come under the influence of Jewish and Christian teachings.

Long before Muhammad's call Arabian paganism was showing signs of decay. At the Ka'aba the Meccans worshipped not only Allah, the supreme Semitic God, but also a number of female deities whom they regarded as the daughters of Allah. Impressed by Jewish and Christian monotheism, a number of spiritual fundamentalists rejected idolatry for an ascetic religion of their own. Muhammad seems to have been influenced by them. He used to go for long, solitary walks, and also to retire to a cave in the mountains in order to give himself up to prayer and meditation.

According to Muslim tradition, one night in Ramadan, about the year AD 611, as he was asleep or in a trance in the cave the Angel Gabriel came to him and said: 'Recite!' He replied: 'What shall I recite?' The order was repeated three times, until the angel himself said:

> Recite: In the name of thy Lord who created –
>   created Man of a blood-clot.
> Recite: And thy Lord is the Most Generous,
> who taught by the Pen, taught Man what he knew not.
>   No, indeed: surely Man waxes insolent,
>   for he thinks himself self-sufficient.
>   Surely unto thy Lord is the Returning.[15]

There can be little doubt that Muhammad was seeking for a vision, actively inducing a trance state by retreating into a cave, which produces a state of sensory deprivation. Being enclosed by the darkness of the cave not only facilitates meditation but

143

reduces the ego awareness of outside reality and produces a hypnoid state which allows the re-emergence of long-forgotten traumas and the emergence of the functions of the id, the unconscious part of the mind, where images and thoughts operate independent of the ego's function and control. The id's experiences evoke the feeling that whatever happens in the mind is independent of the self – it happens. We know that such processes are typical of very small children but can have a powerful influence upon the development of a person and can be brought back to dominance by meditation and the induction of ego loss. Whatever one experiences on the id level does not happen by an act of will or any rational decision: it is a re-emergence of the pre-ego state of the very small child, characterised by the 'omnipotence of thought'. Unconscious wishes or fears obtain a sense of unquestioned reality.

The visions which emerged from Muhammad's mind were a compensation for the deeply-felt loss of his mother and the even more traumatic absence of a father who died before Muhammad was born. He felt the insecurity and anxiety of a void in his mind, the loss of a point of reference, to which he could relate, and the authority of a superego. The ego, the sense of self, was without a guide or direction and left him without purpose or meaning in life. The eternal guide, a centre of reference, had disappeared and as a grown-up a feeling of desolation and loneliness must have haunted him, and he attempted to resurrect it by this self-induced hypnoid trance, when the deep cravings for a father rose to the surface of his mind and acquired the illusion of reality. His dead father comes alive and has the authority and power which he always craved for from a father: he becomes God.

> To God belongs the East and the West, whichever way you turn there is the face of God. He is omnipresent and all knowing, he is what the heaven and the earth contain; all are obedient to

144

Him, creator of the heaven and the earth. When He decrees a thing, he need only say "Be!" and it is!' (Qur'an, Surah II, 115)

Such are the typical manifestations of the omnipotence of thought of young children who believe that whatever they imagine is real before they acquire the capacity of reality testing. If they persist when they grow up and have not developed the ability of the ego to differentiate between fantasy and reality, they are overwhelmed by hallucinations. When the ego and its reality judgment, its distinction between fantasy and reality, is abandoned, it has to submit to hallucination without question or doubt. Beside this psychological condition of Muhammad there was a wider sense of loss of a God of the universe who provides certitude and power to a community or culture among the tribes of the desert, and even among the empires of the Middle East. When Muhammad became acquainted with Jewish and Christian Scriptures he knew that his message would enable him to replace the Jewish and Christian version of God.

He had obviously heard some of the Old Testament and New Testament, but his interpretations are steeped in confusion and misrepresentation. It seems that he had picked up bits from the Bible and retold them according to the way he chose to satisfy his fantasy about the supreme and eternal role of his God, Allah. His stories contradict all logic or even common sense. They are manifestly unreal, like the way a small child tells a story.

[Muhammad reciting the words of Allah]: 'We have bestowed upon the House of Abraham the Book and Wisdom, and We bestowed upon them a mighty dominion.' (IV, 54)

This surely implies that Allah has given to Abraham and his descendants – the Israelites – the Qur'an, which He dictated to Muhammad, His messenger. The problem is that Abraham lived about 1800 BC and Muhammad around AD 600, two thousand four hundred years before Muhammad lived and wrote the

Qur'an. This confusion of time is repeated in the Qur'an – often quite explicitly as a fact, sometimes implicitly inserted in the texts – and is taken for granted, confusing the reader and not allowing him the opportunity to reflect on the absurdity. Muhammad firmly believed he was the messenger of God sent forth to confirm previous Scriptures, which he accused the Jews of having disobeyed and corrupted. He also accused the Christians of worshipping Jesus as the Son of God, although God had expressly commanded to worship none but Him. Having thus gone astray they must be brought back to the right path, which is Islam with its command of unquestioning submission to the will of God. The most important duties of the Muslims are faith in God and his apostle Muhammad, prayer, alms-giving, fasting and pilgrimage to the sacred house of Mecca, built by Abraham for the worship of the One God.

And again,

[Allah speaking to Muhammad]: We made the House [the Ka'aba in Mecca], a resort and a sanctuary for mankind, saying: 'Make the place where Abraham stood a house of worship.' We enjoined Abraham and Ishmael to cleanse Our House for those who walk round it, who meditate in it, and who kneel and prostrate themselves. (Surah II, 125)

However, we must remember that Abraham lived in Haran, which lies in the southern part of the Anatolian highlands, before he was called by God to emigrate to Canaan. Haran is nowhere near Mecca, which is in the Arabian peninsula and more than nine hundred miles away to the south.

The statement in the Qur'an that the sacred house of Allah, the Ka'aba at Mecca, was built by Abraham as a resort and a sanctuary for mankind, and the saying: ' "Make the place where Abraham stood a house of worship." We enjoined Abraham and Ishmael to cleanse our house for those who walk around it, who meditate in it and kneel and prostrate themselves', which is presented as the voice of God – defies the categories of time and space, and has no regard for reality. Abraham is presented as living at the time when the Ka'aba, the sacred shrine of Islam, was built in the seventh century AD, when in historical fact he lived 1800 BC, and the place where he lived was hundreds of miles away. We cannot but consider such statements, presented as holy script, the outpourings of an hallucinatory vision. And furthermore, we cannot ignore the endless repetition of Allah's power and omniscience on every page of the Qur'an, the obsessive description of Him as the Merciful and at the same time His ruthlessness. The obsessive recitation of contradictory slogans, which are presented as the authentic and holy voice of God, not only intend to confuse the reader and overwhelm his rational faculties, but serve to induce an hypnotic effect which overshadows his sense of reality in the same way as Muhammad deliberately wanted to forget reality when he stayed for long periods in caves. He was driven by the urge to resurrect his father, whom he had sorely missed in his childhood and youth, to see him as the all-powerful authority who overcomes all doubt and insecurity. He was obliged to dispense with the criteria of reality and truth to fulfil the desire for a living and powerful father. In the Qur'an we find the endlessly repeated contradictions between the presentation of Allah as the compassionate and merciful and, at the same time, as the angry and vengeful God who is without mercy in his punishment of those who do not believe in him.

The first verses of the Qur'an, Surah II The Cow, read:

In the Name of God, the Compassionate, the Merciful.

This Book is not to be doubted. It is a guide for the righteous who believe in the unseen and are steadfast in prayer; who give in alms from what We gave them; who believe in what has been

147

revealed to you and what was revealed before you, and have absolute faith in the life to come. These are rightly guided by their Lord; these shall surely triumph.

As for the unbelievers, it is the same whether or not you forewarn them; they will not have faith. God has set a seal upon their hearts and ears; their sight is dimmed and grievous punishment awaits them.

The Qur'an, Surah III The Imrans, reads:

There is no god but Him, the Living, the Ever-existent One. He has revealed to you the Book with the Truth, confirming the scriptures which preceded it; for He has already revealed the Torah and the Gospel for the guidance of mankind, and the distinction between right and wrong.

Those that deny God's revelations shall be sternly punished; God is mighty and capable of revenge. Nothing on earth or in heaven is hidden from God. It is He who shapes your bodies in your mothers' wombs as He pleases. There is no god but Him, the Mighty, the Wise One. (1-6)

...

As for the unbelievers, neither their riches nor their children will in the least save them from God's wrath. They shall become the fuel of the Fire. They are like Pharaoh's people, and those before them; they denied Our revelations, and God smote them in their sin. God is stern in retribution.

Say to the unbelievers: 'You shall be overthrown and driven into Hell – an evil resting-place!' (10-12)

It is worthwhile mentioning here that the rules set out in the Qur'an are taught in Islamic schools. The books the students are given speak about idolatry and sin and how to avoid it, about the fires of hell, torture in the grave and how to make sure that your ways are not those of the infidel.

To return to the Qur'an, Surah II The Cow:

How can you deny God? Did He not give you life when you

were dead, will He not cause you to die and then restore you to life? Will you not return to Him at last? (28)

Surah III The Imrans, reads:

God bears witness that there is no god but Him and so do the angels and the sages. He is the Executor of Justice, the Only God, the Mighty, the Wise One. The only true faith in God's sight is Islam. Those to whom the Scriptures were given disagreed amongst themselves, through insolence, only after knowledge had been vouchsafed them. He that denies God's revelation should know that swift is God's reckoning. (18-19)

God said: 'Jesus, I am about to claim you back and lift you up to Me. I shall take you away from the unbelievers and exalt your followers above them till the Day of Resurrection. Then to Me you shall all return and I shall judge your disputes. The unbelievers shall be sternly punished in this world and in the world to come: there shall be none to help them. As for those that have faith and do good works, they shall be given their reward in full. God does not love the evildoers.'
This revelation, and this wise admonition, We recite to you. Jesus is like Adam in the sight of God. He created him from dust and then said to him: 'Be,' and he was. (55-59)

He that chooses a religion other than Islam, it will not be accepted from him, and in the world to come he will surely be among the losers. (85)

Believers, if you yield to the infidels they will drag you back to unbelief and you will return headlong to perdition. (149)

Surah XXII Pilgrimage, reads:

You people, have fear of the Lord. The catastrophe of the Hour of Doom shall be terrible indeed. When that day comes, every suckling mother shall forsake her infant, every pregnant female shall cast her burden, and you shall see mankind reeling like drunkards, although not drunk: such shall be the horror of God's chastisement. (1-3)

The Hour of Doom is sure to come – of this there is no doubt. Those who are in their graves God will raise to life. (XXII, 6)

Surah CX Help, reads:

In the Name of God, the Merciful, the Compassionate.
When God's help and victory comes, and you see men embrace God's faith in multitudes, give glory to the Lord and seek His pardon. He is ever disposed to mercy.

Surah CXI Perish, reads:

In the Name of God, the Merciful, the Compassionate.
May the hands of Abu-Lahab [the prophet's uncle and one of his opponents] perish! May he himself perish! Nothing shall his wealth and gains avail him. He shall be burnt in a flaming fire, and his wife, laden with firewood, shall have a rope of fibre around her neck!

Surah IV Women, reads:

These are the bounds set by Allah. Allah will make the man who obeys Allah and His messenger enter the Gardens beneath which rivers flow. He will abide there for ever. That is the mighty triumph. And he who disobeys Allah and His messenger and transgresses the bounds set by Him – him shall Allah cause to enter the Fire. There he will abide. A humiliating chastisement awaits him. (13-14)

In the second volume of *Towards Understanding the Qur'an*, the editor Zafar Ishaq Ansari comments upon this surah: 'This is a terrifying verse in which those who tamper with God's laws, laid down by God in His Book, are warned of unending punishment. It is lamentable that, in spite of these very stern warnings, Muslims have occasionally been guilty of breaching God's laws with the same boldness and insolence as that of the Jews.' [16]

The first followers of Muhammad were a small group: a few young members of the leading families of Quraysh, together with members of other tribes who had come to them for protection, and also some less privileged people. But as support for him grew, the leading families cooled towards him; they began to see him not as a messenger from God, but as one who attacked their way of life. They complained to his uncle, Abu Talib, saying, 'Your nephew has cursed our gods, insulted our religion, mocked our way of life and accused our forefathers of error.' And things became even worse for Muhammad when both his uncle and his wife died in AD 619.

As it became more apparent how the new ideas of Islam differed from paganism, his supporters began to attack the local idols of the gods and pagan ceremonies, and to demand new forms of worship. At this time Muhammad saw himself as being in the tradition of the Jewish and Christian prophets.

Eventually matters became so difficult for him that he went to Medina, an oasis some two hundred miles to the north of Mecca. It was easier than it might have been for him to establish his religious authority in Medina, as the Jews who lived there had been guided by the prophets of the Bible, and local tradesmen had also been prepared to accept this way of solving disputes. Since Muhammad saw himself as a prophet, too, he was able to come to agreements with all parties living in the area, and now tribal disputes, which had been settled by force, were to be judged by 'God and Muhammad'.

At Medina, Muhammad began to gain power over a wide area. He and his supporters had to fight with the Quraysh and with Mecca; it is possible that this was over trade routes, but the struggle consolidated his ideas and the shape of his community who came to believe that they were fighting for God against the insolence of the Quraysh. It is no surprise, then, that Muhammad's teaching took on a more universal quality, looking to the wider world and separating itself from Judaism and Christianity.

Initially, Muhammad and the Jews were on good terms, as they all accepted the authority of the Bible. But as his claims grew, the relationship became strained. The Jews could not accept him as a prophet within their tradition, and Muhammad for his part accused them of perverting their own tradition. Matters ended in the murder or expulsion of the Jews.

Having thus suppressed the Jewish voice, Muhammad placed a new emphasis on his spiritual descent from Abraham, whom he saw as neither Jewish nor Christian, but as the common ancestor of all three beliefs. Abraham was declared the founder of a monotheistic faith with Mecca – not Jerusalem – as its centre, which henceforth should be faced in prayer.

Muhammad believed that his vision of Allah as the supreme God of the universe could be reified in the world, and when opportunities presented themselves he took full advantage of them. An important one came about in Mecca, where trade routes were under threat and alliances between tribal chiefs and merchants were not as stable as previously. Muslims in the city felt at risk for as long as the ruling classes of Mecca were hostile to them; and yet at the same time their numbers were increasing, so they wished for an end to the hostility. Muhammad's vision and skills brought about a reconciliation between the various parties and the city came under his and Islamic control.

However, he kept Medina as his capital, and there his way of governing was to exercise authority by political manipulation and personal ascendancy rather than by regular government. Some of the many marriages he made during this time were entered into for reasons of political expediency.

Muhammad was influential over a wide area, where he brought peace to quarrelling tribal chiefs through his control of the oases and markets, and took on the role of supreme arbiter.

He made different sorts of agreements with different people. In some, there was friendship and peace; in others he demanded that the people accept him as prophet, and as a concomitant, the obligation to pray and to make financial contributions. These might be military levies or voluntary gifts.[17]

On the last occasion when he visited Mecca, in AD 632, the year of his death, Muhammad made his definitive statement: 'Know that every Muslim is a Muslim's brother, and that he will fight until all men should confess, "There is no God but God."'

His followers were momentarily thrown into confusion when he died. Abu Bakr, one of their leaders, proclaimed, 'O men, if you worship Muhammad, Muhammad is dead, if you worship God, God is alive.'

Muhammad had claimed universal authority; that the *haram* he established had no natural limits. Towards the end of his life, he sent out military expeditions against the Byzantine frontiers, and ambassadors to the great rulers, calling on them to embrace Islam. Upon his death, however, his alliances threatened to break up, some of the tribal chiefs refused to accept him as the Prophet or rejected the Islamic political control of Medina.

His adherents, first under Abu Bakr, were not prepared to accept this situation, and took to arms. By AD 644 the whole of Arabia, the Syrian and Egyptian parts of the Byzantine empire, and some of the Sasanian empire had been overcome. The remaining Sasanian lands were taken soon afterwards.

The Islamic conquerors exercised control from armed camps, whether in established cities or in new settlements which themselves gradually grew into cities: Basra and Kufa in Iraq; Fustat (later Cairo) in Egypt. Each of them had a governor's palace, and at the city centre, a mosque, where all could meet.

In the 690s Arabic became the language of government, and new Islamic coins were issued. In 690 a great building was erected to assert the distinct and enduring nature of Islam, namely the Dome of the Rock, built on the ancient site of the Jewish Temple in Jerusalem where, according to Jewish teaching, God had called upon Abraham to sacrifice his son Isaac. This site now became a Muslim *haram* where pilgrims met, and Islam had a new symbol of its power.[18]

3. THE LIBRARY OF ALEXANDRIA AND THE REDISCOVERY OF GREEK PHILOSOPHY.

When Egypt was conquered by the Arabs in 641 Alexandria was still a centre of Greek philosophy. An extraordinary passion for the translation of Greek philosophers of the Classical period permeated the town originally founded by Alexander the Great. Of its estimated population of one million people something like 200,000 were Jewish. Greek, Jewish and Christian scholars were dedicated to the task of translation, categorising and interpreting the great works of Athens, and provide the most inspiring commentaries.

After the destruction of the Temple of Jerusalem by the Romans a great number of Jewish philosophers turned to Alexandria, encouraged by the free spirit of enquiry which pervaded the city. Many Christians were fascinated by a philosophy which upheld the idea of the unity of the spirit that unites humanity in the fatherhood of God. This was of course the main principle of monotheism as expounded by the Jewish prophets.

When Justinian closed the School of Athens (AD 529), Greek philosophers found a refuge in Alexandria, whose fame was widespread by that time. It was already flourishing as the centre of Greek philosophy, medicine and science and attracted many Muslim thinkers determined to produce a fresh spiritual foundation for Islam in response to the conflicts which had beset it.

Alexandria became the centre of a renewed interpretation of

the religious systems which came together in the city. Intellectuals among the ancient religions of the Hebrews and the Christians and then the Muslims were inspired by Greek philosophy's contribution to the perennial question of what is truth: how do we find the answer to the relation of the human intellect to the concept of God, the universal power behind the flux of events in the world around us? And there developed a co-operation among the Jews, Christians and Muslims in the translation of the writings of the Greek philosophers. Alexandria brought the Arabs into contact with the culture of Greece. Among the most important translations were the works of Plato, particularly his *Timaeus* in Galen's synopsis of that great dialogue, Aristotle's *De anima, Analytica priora,* and the apocryphal *Secret of Secrets* (ascribed to Aristotle) during the reign of Harun al-Rashid (786-809).

As controversy grew over the questions of free will, divine justice and the meaning of the Divine texts in the Bible, and the Qur'an in particular, theologians felt a growing need to turn to philosophy and logic for the refinement of their concepts and methods of proof. However, a certain antipathy to Greek philosophy, because of its pagan origins, began to surface in theological quarters.

Nevertheless, philosophy would receive the enthusiastic support of distinguished scholars and authors. They were fascinated by the Neo-Platonic world-view of the philosopher Plotinus and his concept of the utter transcendence of the Supreme Being and the noble destiny it promised to those who unreservedly devoted themselves to it. This brand of late Greek philosophy was a brilliant attempt to bring together the major currents in Classical Greek thought, Platonic, Aristotelian, Pythagorean and Stoic. It is not surprising that this should capture the imagination of Muslim philosophers, as shown by the fact that among the first philosophical texts to be translated into Arabic was a summary of the last three books of Plotinus' *Enneads*. However, the great works of Aristotle as well as the synopses of Plato's *Sophist*, *Parmenides*, the *Republic* and the *Laws*, Aristotle's *Categories*, *Hermeneutica*, the *Nicomachean Ethics*, and parts of the *Physics* were translated and distributed in many centres of Syria, Iraq, Persia and Arabia.

Despite the appeal of Plotinus to Islamic theology, many Islamic philosophers such as al-Kindi (died c. 866), who was as anxious to defend the Qur'anic view as he was the Greek, and al-Razi (died c. 925), were far closer to Plato than to Plotinus, while others, like Ibn Rushd (died 1198) regarded Aristotle as the paragon of wisdom.

Despite their community of purpose in the pursuit and the elucidation of religious truth, the philosophers and theologians were increasingly at loggerheads; the Aristotelian world-view with its twin principles of causality – everything that is must have a cause for its being, and the uniformity of nature which 'does nothing in vain', as Aristotle put it – appeared to Islamic theologians inimical to the Qur'anic view of the world. According to this, God can effect His designs in the world imperiously and miraculously without any impediments or restraints upon His unlimited power. Nor is He answerable for any of His actions.

Following its flowering in the East during the tenth and eleventh centuries, philosophy received major reverses at the hands of Asharite, Hanbalite and Literalist theologians and scholars of Islam. The areas of study derived from Greek philosophy became known as foreign sciences and were treated with suspicion by the pious. In the twelfth century Baghdad scholars and theologians formed a consensus to forbid debate within Islam. They thought that all this debate and dissent within Islam would cause it to fall apart.[19]

As a consequence of the reverses they received in the Muslim world of the East, philosophers sought a refuge in the Western parts of the Muslim empire.

The Arabs first landed in Spain, al-Andalus, as they called it, in the eighth century when the Umayyads had founded a dynasty, and before long they were able to rival the Abbasids of the east, not only politically but culturally.

The historian of medicine and philosophy, Sa'id al-Andalusi, who lived and wrote in Spain, said that while the study of Greek philosophy and medicine in al-Andalus had started in the reign of the Umayyad Caliph Muhammad Ibn 'Abd al-Rahman' (852-866) interest in the subjects had been renewed in the tenth century. This was when Baghdad and Cordoba were the intellectual centres of Islam.

In eleventh-century Spain, the foundations were being laid for a genuine philosophical and scientific revolution which would embrace and revive Aristotelian philosophy and which heralded the movement of Greek-Arabic philosophy to the west. The philosophy of the Greeks had been almost lost to Europe since the time when Boethius (d. 525) had translated Aristotle into Latin, enabling people to read his work. But not until Ibn Rushd's commentaries had also been translated, much later, did the revival of philosophy in Western Europe truly begin.

There is no doubt that Ibn Rushd, known in the West as Averroes, was the supreme figure in philosophy in al-Andalus. He was born in Cordoba in 1126, and until he was forty, he studied medicine and jurisprudence. At this point he met the Caliph Abu Ya'qub Yusuf, who was keen to gain a fuller understanding of Aristotle, and who invited Ibn Rushd to explain his work to him. Ibn Rushd's polymathy is demonstrated by the fact that he was also appointed chief judge of Cordoba in 1171 and royal physician to the court of Marrakesh in 1182. He produced extensive commentaries on the works of Aristotle, and made Plato's *Republic* available in a paraphrase. He was also very

157

critical of the position taken by the powerful representative of the theological world-view within Islam, the theologian al-Ghazali (1058-1111), who worked in Baghdad. As head of the Nizamiyah School, al-Ghazali taught Islamic jurisprudence and theology. He deeply disapproved of philosophical dissent, which was why Ibn Rushd was so critical of his work. [20]

Al-Ghazali's legacy is that he made an assessment of Greek-Arabic philosophy from an Islamic perspective. We know from his autobiography that he spent three years studying writings in this field in considerable depth. He notes that at the end of this time 'I was able, through divine assistance and the mere perusal of their books, to grasp the pith of their sciences.' But his aim was to refute philosophy in favour of theology, not least by showing that philosophers were infidel or heretical. In furtherance of this end, his most important point was that philosophers restrict the scope of God's knowledge so much that 'the Lord of Lords and Cause of Causes has no knowledge of what happens in the world', even though in Islamic theology God created the world through His knowledge and will. Al-Ghazali supports this point by saying that the Qur'an states that 'not a single atom's weight in the heavens or on earth is hidden from Him.' Al-Ghazali further sets out to indicate 'the consensus of all Muslims' that there cannot be any limits to the way in which He can operate freely in the world of which He is the Supreme Lord.

Al-Ghazali would not admit the claim of the philosophers that it is from the intellect and its exercise that we arrive at an understanding of God's purpose and the nature of the universe by the principle that everything that is must have a cause for its being, for this principle contradicts the teaching of the Qur'an which shows that God and the world He has created has no Cause but is the expression of His Will alone, that gave birth to the universe and everything it contains, including mankind and the human mind. God only has to say 'Be!' and it will be. [21]

Philosophers, however, take it as the starting-point of their endeavours to explain the causes for everything that exists, including the mind, and attempt to discover the modes and categories of thought. This, in the view of Islamic teaching, separates men from the union with God and fundamentally contradicts the spirit of the Qur'an.

While Ibn Rushd became the leader of the Western Muslim world and indeed one of the great contributors to Western philosophy, al-Ghazali led Islam to embrace an anti-philosophical theology that became enshrined in the growing multitude of madrassas which taught the complete and unreserved submission to the authority and truths of the holy script of the Qur'an and the duty to resist the teachings of philosophers and Western civilisation.

In the battle between the two world-views, Ibn Rushd's strategy was to show that the disagreement between Islam and the philosophers was not so radical as to justify the charge of infidelity levelled against the philosophers by the theologians. This did not, however, affect their determination to outlaw any further incursion of philosophical debate amongst Muslims in order to preserve the purity of the Qur'anic teachings on the universal and unlimited power of Allah in all its manifestations, which includes the life of mankind. The Islamic theologians set up an expanding number of madrassas, teaching academies, which also operated in the mosques, with mullahs and imams as the ordained teachers of the true faith. They felt it to be their duty and their calling to extend them over the world, proclaiming Islam as the only and supreme faith.

While the Andalusian school of philosophy flourished for about three centuries, it had come to an end with the reconquest of Spain by the Christian kingdoms of Leon and Castile in the

159

thirteenth century, finally completed with the fall of Cordoba (1236). The Muslims were expelled and had to flee, and settled on the northern shores of Africa where many became prominent physicians and mathematicians, noted for the discovery of algebra and trigonometry. Most Jewish philosophers remained in Spain and continued to be major contributors to the spread of philosophy in the Western world, playing an important role in the emergence of the Renaissance in the West. This, however, did not save them from the Inquisition.

Thus the golden age of Islam came to an end. The religion of Islam was forced to return to the Middle Ages, and remained there, with very few exceptions.

Before I describe the different ways in which Islam and the West developed after the fourteenth century, I want to come back to the Christian Middle Ages and show its similarity to the nature of Islamic teaching up to present times. The religious and political beliefs imposed by the Christian Church bear many similarities, indeed, are almost identical, with the state of mind and beliefs of Islam.

While Christianity inherited the monotheistic concept of the whole man – the uniqueness of his mind and his body – and God's intention that human beings should develop their full potential, it transformed man into a being that was half beast and half angel, as Feuerbach remarked. The Western world rediscovered the spirit of Classical Athens and freed itself from unquestioning submission to religious dogma; the East denied itself the opportunity to rediscover the Greek Narcissus, the love of the body and the mind and its God-given potential to explore the secret and the beauty of Nature, both around him and in him.

The irony of this is that while the Arabs together with the Jews provided the West with the inspiration of Athenian philosophy and opened up the message of humanism to the world, their Islamic brothers refuse to drink from the well of wisdom they had discovered by declaring philosophical questions anathema to the true faith of Islam. This has made it impossible for them to develop and refine their ideas and participate in the transformation brought about in the Western world, leaving them behind in the astonishing progress made by the West. The true Muslim is he who has faith simply to submit to the revealed God and to act in accordance with His will. Within the Muslim community controversies and speculation which will lead to dissension and conflict must be avoided.

In order to show the similarity between the Christian Middle Ages and the beliefs of Islam which have continued unchanged up to our time, I shall quote a few lines from my earlier chapter on Christianity. I wrote:

'Augustine represents the radical transformation from the human optimism of the Classical world to the despondent passivity of the Middle Ages. The mentality he expressed was to become the dominant outlook of Christianity and to encompass the whole of European society for many centuries. Christianity gave Europe some fragments of Jewish law, a thing which the Jews with their appeal to moral discipline would hardly have been able to do, but the cost of this was the universalisation of a split mind. By introducing the concept of original sin, Christianity intensified man's guilt about his natural self to a degree unknown in any previous religion. Nature became evil and had to be conquered within man and around him. But the nature which exists in man does not cease to function, indeed, cannot cease to function; it becomes split off from the self and projected upon 'the others', where it operates as a constant threat. God himself became an enemy of the natural man, of man's nature, and he became ever more frightening, so that man could only relate to him through the mediation of Jesus. Without his mediation man was doomed, the inevitable victim of God's wrath.

161

Thus the Church, as the representative of Jesus, could present itself as the only source of man's salvation and its claim of total power was unquestionable.

'The history of the Church was for Augustine', the author of *City of God*, 'the march of God in the world... and human life is the theatre of a cosmic struggle between the goodness of God and the evil of rebellious spirits.' Augustine maintained that the powers that be in the Christian empire are ordained by God and that the use of force was made necessary by sin and as the divinely appointed remedy for sin. Henceforth human salvation is bound up with the interests of the Church represented by the kings appointed by it, and these interests are in consequence paramount over all other interests whatsoever. [22]

The intellectual father of modern Islamism, Sayyid Abul A'la Mawdudi (1903-1979), claimed that Islam is entirely self-sufficient, being God's final revelation to humankind, and supersedes all other religions and philosophies. He believed that the law had been revealed to Muhammad for all time and for all humanity. Mawdudi argued that *jihad* was the ultimate political struggle for the whole of mankind:

> Islam is not concerned with the interests of one nation to the exclusion of others and does not intend to elevate one people to the exclusion of others. It is not at all interested in what state rules and dominates the earth, but only in the happiness and welfare of humanity. Therefore Islam resists any government that is based on a different concept and programme, in order to liquidate it completely. Its aim is to make this concept victorious, to introduce this programme universally, to set up governments that are firmly rooted in this concept and this programme, irrespective of who carries the banner of truth and justice, or whose flag of aggression and corruption is thereby toppled. Islam wants the whole earth and does not content itself with only a part thereof. It wants and requires the entire inhabited world.

Mawdudi's writings became available in Arabic translation during the 1950s. [23]

Besides the obsession with conquest in the name of their respective God, the Christians of the Middle Ages and modern Islam share a preoccupation with death with its promises of heavenly paradise or the torture of hell, and a fear of women.

Medieval man had lost the image of the human being that unites in himself both the divine spirit as well as the forces of nature, and encompasses the manifold of desires and aspirations for an overriding purpose of life. The earth and all human existence were seen to be in a state of suspension between two eternal realms where the demons and devils of the underworld constantly clamour to take possession of the mind and bodies of men in their earthly existence and can only be warded off by Christ on the cross or submission to Allah. Earthly existence is pervaded by sinful desires and pursuits, while the renunciation of a sinful existence would promise the blessing of heaven, the state of beatitude in the love of Jesus or Allah. Prayers for forgiveness and rituals of submitting to His will had to be observed in order to gain the right of entry into heaven. Thus the renunciation of earthly desires and the desire for death would be a pervasive state of mind and assurance to Allah that the believers are prepared to give up the life on earth in order to gain the right of entry into the heavenly paradise.

In the thirteenth and fourteenth century Christianity was ruled by a preoccupation with death, but while the Christians were afraid of it and of purgatory for their sinful existences, Muslims increasingly looked with equanimity and even desire for the possibility of entering paradise, and were ready to sacrifice their life to assure the blessing of a heavenly paradise and the love of Allah.

Again: man has lost the image of the human being that unites in himself both the divine spirit as well as the forces of nature and encompasses the manifold desires and aspirations into an overriding purpose of life, which was God's intention.

The fear of human nature is exemplified by the sin of sexual desire which became manifest in the epidemic of witch-hunts. The witch was either the good, sexually repressed Christian woman, or the utterly uninhibited lover of Satan flaunting all kinds of sexual perversions. In the fourteenth century, epidemics of witch-hunts and large-scale trials and executions of witches took place all over Europe. Every woman became suspect of having links with the forces of darkness and of plotting against the Church. Conversely, every Christian woman was in danger of being seduced by the Evil One. The anxious preoccupation with the possibility of their women being tempted and seduced by the devil was the consequence of the repressed male fear of sexuality. While the libido has been split off from the ego of the good Christian and projected upon the devil, the woman had been attracted to him and he would play a lively and dangerous role in her erotic fantasy; she would rebel against the God who denies her natural instincts and ally herself to His enemies.

Once again we find men's fears of women's sexual desires, tempting men to surrender to the sinful urges of nature, continued in Islam, where the men have to protect themselves from sexual desires of their women by insisting that their bodies are covered from head to toe by wearing the *burkha*. Their voices must not be heard in public, they are not allowed to express their thoughts and opinions, nor are they in any way to participate in public affairs, in politics or in religious worship. Not even in their home must she be seen undressed. Their very nature as women – their feminine characteristics, their personalities – has to be hidden to protect men from its dangers.

The woman's role in life is to procreate and multiply and produce offspring, particularly sons dedicated to serving Allah and spreading God's message among men, to fight and subdue the infidel.

Whereas the Christians build nunneries where women can choose to serve God and renounce their sexual desires, the Muslims do not trust women to do so voluntarily and impose the taboo of sexuality on women generally and strict control over them.

(It is curious that I have never been able to find a command in the Qur'an that women have to wear a *burkha*, even while men's supremacy is repeatedly stressed. It seems to me that the wearing of the *burkha* was imposed as a supreme duty by the imams and ayatollahs of the Islamic establishment, in order to increase their powers as the saviours from the dangers of sin.)

4. ISLAM DIVIDED

Despite the proclamation of Islam that its God and its religion is bound forever by its unity of belief and worship, it has historically been divided into two opposing beliefs. This split in Islam was dramatically initiated by the victory of its church, namely by the Baghdad theologians led by al-Ghazali who insisted upon a break with the philosophers. It split Islam into two opposing camps and imposed the dogmas of the Eastern theologians as the only true faith. This made it impossible for Islam to develop and to refine its ideas, and it fell behind in the intellectual as well as social progress of the Western world. It put an end to the golden age of Islam when its intellectuals discovered the writings of the Greek philosophers and attempted to resurrect the belief in the One and universal God who not only created the universe and humanity and endowed it with the capacity for rational thought but gave man a brain able to explore the world He had created, to choose between right and wrong, good and bad, and to come to understand the aims and purposes He has in mind for humanity. Therefore philosophic enquiry and scientific investigation are an intrinsic part of human beings which God wants his latest and supreme creation to exercise to its fullest potential in its development towards maturity.

In denying these God-given faculties in men, the spokesmen of Islamic authority also contradict God's intentions and purposes when they prohibit the teachings of its philosophers. They not only have created a split within Islam, but also present a split image of God who has created man with a multiplicity and diversity of faculties, a capacity to investigate the truth of his beliefs by the exercise of reason, logic and empirical evidence, an ability to ask questions, to discuss and argue, and the freedom to exercise his rational faculties. He has endowed man with a brain that has many aspects, but the latest of its God-given capacities is the exercise of the pre-frontal lobes, which have the ability of foresight and the anticipation of the consequences of actions, and to assess and to control the more primitive areas of the mind dominated by instinct-driven reflexes and irrational beliefs and prejudices. He wants mankind to grow up and exercise and affirm the latest and most recent faculties which God has given it, which set it apart from the animal kingdom and gave it a decisive advantage in the competition with other species: to ask why things happen and why it thinks and acts in a certain way, and to ask God to guide it and to discuss with Him. God has given man a brain and a mind, with the ability to reason and to reflect upon the purpose of life, and learn to think for himself, and not like a child to depend upon a divine authority, an omnipotent and omniscient father to think for it. The God who created man wants him to learn to understand God's designs, and to recreate paradise in the world by his own efforts, in the fulfilment of his maturity.

5. IBN RUSHD AND PICO DELLA MIRANDOLA

Among the Muslims it was Ibn Rushd as well as other philosophers who proclaimed the unification of reason and belief, of rational as well as moral values; among the Christians of the Middle Ages it was Pico della Mirandola who did this and opened a new vista for humanity.

After the oppressive rule of the mediaeval Church, the drive towards maturity, for freedom and self-respect could not be denied forever. The forgotten doctrine of man's holiness as a creation of God as propounded by Jewish monotheism and the Platonic theory of man's innate capability to comprehend the truth were brought to Europe by Jewish and Arab scholars, and they contributed greatly towards the reawakening of the concept of humanity and of the universal man. Men strove to rehabilitate the body, the senses, the heart and the intelligence, and they rekindled the fascination for nature. Men began to rediscover the unity of man and nature and man's being as a form of nature chosen by God to fulfil His purpose.

The conception of man's humanity was proclaimed by Pico della Mirandola in his essay *On the Dignity of Man*. God, he tells us, made man at the close of the creation to know the laws of the universe, to love its beauty, to admire its greatness. 'I have set thee,' says the Creator to Adam, 'in the midst of the world, that thou mayest the more easily behold and see all that is therein. To thee alone is given a growth and a development depending on thine own free will. Thou bearest in thee the germs of a universal life.' [24]

Pico della Mirandola (1463-1494) read Plato in Greek and Moses in Hebrew. When the sacred writings from Jerusalem mingled with the philosophy of the Greeks and were transplanted together upon the soil of fifteenth century Italy, a new flower grew from it unlike any flower men had seen before.

167

In proclaiming the harmony between Plato and Moses, Pico imbues every natural object with a higher meaning as an analogue to a divine purpose. The Jewish cosmology, governed by a moral purpose and the Platonic concept of human reason combined to produce an image of humanity which is not a helpless victim of the cosmic conflict between good and evil but a being who, in his freedom to exercise his innate potentials, is capable of fulfilling God's aim in the world.

Emancipation from the authority of the Church and liberation from its mental shackles led to an astonishing display of genius in the arts and in literature and in the unfolding of the multiplicity of human sensibilities. While the individual was free to explore nature and the human being in both its intellectual as well as aesthetic aspects, while the universe became the roving ground of the mind, this did not lead to the establishment of universalistic doctrines or dogmas of which there had been a surfeit during the Middle Ages.

The Italian Renaissance spread to Germany mainly due to the friendship between Pico della Mirandola and the German scholar Johannes Reuchlin. The young Italian philosopher became the teacher of Reuchlin, his inspiration and model, and it was largely through Reuchlin that the great ideas of the Renaissance spread into Germany and eventually developed into the ideas of the Enlightenment.

Encouraged by Pico della Mirandola, Reuchlin entered into a systematic study of Hebrew and the original texts of the Old Testament; in particular, it was the Cabbala that aroused his interests. On his return to Germany he began to advocate the introduction of Hebraic studies in German universities, as well as the study of the Greek language and Greek literature. While he managed to establish courses in Greek studies at the universities of Stuttgart and Heidelberg, his efforts on behalf of Hebrew aroused furious opposition from the Church. It was, however, not merely the new ideas which he had propagated but the fanatical opposition of the Church and his persecution by the Inquisition which created a stir among German scholars and for a time made him the rallying-point of the new movement. The efforts of the inquisitors to secure Reuchlin's fall appeared to be so fanatical and ignorant as to drive most of the German humanists into sympathy with Reuchlin and contempt for his opponents. They considered the ban on Hebrew books a threat against the basic values of humanism. The meeting of northern scholarship with the Italian humanistic Renaissance was bound to have a powerful impact upon the development of European culture; it was like opening a window and looking out into the wider new world that had emerged in Italy in the previous two centuries.

Encouraged by the Italian Renaissance and the Old Testament (translated by Luther and made widely available through the printing press), with its sanctification of life on earth as the creation of God, men began to feel free to turn their curiosity to the material world and to the shaping, handling and manipulating of nature to make it give forth wealth and to reveal its secrets. Work became a redeeming activity, a form of salvation; it became a virtue and the wealth produced a symbol of man's self-realisation. While in the ancient religions surplus products were offered to the gods on altars, and burnt and cooked for their consumption, the wealth of the Protestant was given over to making better machines, bigger workshops and factories, new inventions and the organisations of accounting houses and banks: these were the altars of God.

Benjamin Franklin based his puritan work ethic upon the Old Testament, and in particular on a passage which his Calvinistic father drummed into him again and again as a youth: 'Seest thou a man diligent in his enterprise? He shall stand before kings' (*Proverbs* xxii, 29). However, we see here a signifi-

169

cant difference between the puritan denial of pleasure and the Jew's right to enjoy the fruits of his labours so long as he shows his gratitude and gives thanks to God.

By searching for the unifying principle behind the phenomena, the Renaissance philosopher attempted to get nearer to the creator and understand his mind and purpose. This belief in the power of human reason is linked with the doctrine of human dignity and the belief in a God who is near to men and wants men to learn to be rational, responsible and creative beings. Conversely, the denial of this belief in the power of human reason is almost invariably linked with distrust of men.

In religions where God deems us to be sinful and degraded, he does not expect us to understand things, and we remain dependent on dogma. If God loves us he wants us to know and understand; he equips us with the capacity for knowledge and with an intellect by which we can comprehend his creations. In psychoanalytic terms, we witness a transformation from a distrustful and distant superego, afraid of men's evil nature and determined to make them submit to its will and commandments, to a superego that is friendly and trustful of men's innate goodness. The new image of the universal Father encourages and teaches men to develop their moral and intellectual potentials, and the ancient hostility between father and sons is to be resolved by their mutual love and respect. And in the love of God the Father we learn and become able to love each other.

Notes to Islam.

[1] Extracted from the article by Anthony Browne: The triumph of the East, *The Spectator* 24 July 2004, paragraphs 6-9.

[2] *Genesis* xvi, 1-2, 4-6. Author's note: I use the names 'Abraham' and 'Sarah' throughout this whole extract rather than 'Abram' and 'Sarai', as given up to Chapter xvii, 5 and xvii, 15 respectively.

[3] *Genesis* xxi, 10-14, with a little rephrasing in verse 11; and then as follows:

[4] xxi, 16-18;

[5] xxi, 20 and xvii, 25. A little rephrasing, and verses concertinaed.

[6] xvii, 20;

[7] xvii, 15-21;

[8] xviii, 10-12, 14;

[9] xxi, 1-4, verse 3 a little rephrased.

[10] *See* Dan Brown: *The Da Vinci Code*, Chapter 55.

[11] *See* A. H. M. Jones: *Constantine and the Conversion of Europe*, Chapter 10: The Council of Nicaea.

[12] *Ibid.* Chapter 16: Constantine's Place in History.

[13] *See* Albert Hourani: *A History of the Arab Peoples*, Chapter 1.

[14] *Ibid.*

[15] The Qur'an, XCVI The Blood-Clot, 1-8.

[16] Sayyid Abul A'la Mawdudi: *Towards Understanding the Qur'an*, Vol. 2, edited and translated by Zafar Ishaq Ansari, pp. 16-17.

[17] *See* Albert Hourani: Chapter 1.

[18] *Ibid.* Chapter 2.

[19] *See* Majid Fakhry: *Islamic Philosophy, Theology and Mysticism*, Introduction and Chapter 1.

[20] *Ibid.* Chapter 7.

[21] *Ibid.* Chapter 5.

[22] *See* pp. 109-110, and p. 108 above. *See* also George Frankl: *The Social History of the Unconscious*, Chapter 9.

[23] Malise Ruthven: *A Fury for God*, Chapter 2: Jihad, pp. 68, 70-71.

[24] *See* George Frankl: *The Social History of the Unconscious*, Chapter 10.

Epilogue

Mankind suffers from an instinctual void; we are never quite sure what we have to do, not being conditioned in our actions and impulses by the certainty of instinct. However, the genius of human beings is that we are equipped with the ability to choose – with the freedom to choose between right and wrong, what is good and bad, to anticipate the result of our actions, and to see ourselves doing things before we actually do them and discriminate which ones are of advantage for our survival and our well-being as a species and as individuals. This genius is given to us by the ability of the prefrontal lobes of our brains to discriminate between what serves our needs and what is detrimental to our survival.

But the instinctual void makes it necessary for us to be taught what is right for us as members of our species; we need models and teachers to guide us and instruct us. Hence the quest for the eternal and omnipotent guide and the quest for universal values: the search for God.

List of Biblical Quotations

List of Surahs cited

Selected Bibliography

Arberry, A. J: *The Koran Interpreted*, OUP, *World's Classics*, 1975.

Armstrong, Karen: *Islam* A Short History, Phoenix Press, 2001.

Augustine of Hippo: *City of God*, Penguin Classics, 1972.

Badcock, C. R: *The Psychoanalysis of Culture*, Basil Blackwell, Oxford, 1980.

Bible, The Holy, Authorised King James Version, OUP; *see also Revised Standard Version*.

The Book of Common Prayer, OUP.

Bousset, Wilhelm: *Die Religion des Judentums*, J. C. B. Mohr, 1966.

Brandon, S. G. F: *Jesus and the Zealots*, Manchester, 1967.

Brod, Max: *Johannes Reuchlin*, W. Kohlhammer, Stuttgart, 1965.

Burckhardt, J: *The Civilisation of the Renaissance in Italy*, Phaidon, 1965.

Dawood, N. J: *The Koran*, Penguin Classics, 1956, 1999.

Dimont, Max: *The Indestructible Jews*, New American Library, 1971.

Dodd, C. H: *The Interpretation of the Fourth Gospel*, CUP, 1970.

Fakhry, Majid: *Islamic Philosophy, Theology and Mysticism – A Short Introduction*, Oneworld, Oxford, 1997, 2003.

Feiler, Bruce: *Abraham* – In Search of the Father of Civilisation, Piatkus, 2002.

Frankl, George: *The End of War or the End of Mankind*, Globe Publications, 1955.

— *The Failure of the Sexual Revolution*, Kahn & Averill, 1974; Nel Mentor Classics, 1975; Open Gate Press, 2004.

— *The Social History of the Unconscious – A Psychoanalysis of Society*, Open Gate Press, 1990, 2002.
Available also in 2 volumes, as:
— *Archaeology of the Mind*, Open Gate Press, 1992.
— *Civilisation: Utopia and Tragedy*, Open Gate Press, 1992.

— *The Unknown Self*, Open Gate Press, 1990, 1993, 2001.

— *Exploring the Unconscious*, Open Gate Press, 1994, 2001.

— *Foundations of Morality*, Open Gate Press, 2000, 2001.

— *Blueprint for a Sane Society*, Open Gate Press, 2004.

181

Freud, Sigmund: *Moses and Monotheism*, Standard Edition XXIII.
— 'Dostoyevsky and Parricide', Standard Edition XXI, 185.
Graves, Robert and Podro, Joshua: *The Nazarene Gospel Restored*, Cassell, 1953.
Grayzel, Solomon: *A History of the Jews*, Mentor, NAL, 1968.
Hayes, John H. and J. Maxwell Miller (Eds.) *Israelite and Judean History*, Old Testament Library, SCM Press, 1977.
Hourani, Albert: *A History of the Arab Peoples*, Faber & Faber, 1991.
Huizinga, Johan: *The Waning of the Middle Ages*, Pelican, 1972.
The Interpreter's Dictionary of the Bible, An Illustrated Encyclopedia in Four Volumes, Ed. G. A. Buttrick, Abingdon Press, 1962.
Johnson, Paul: *The History of Christianity*, A Peregrine Book published by Penguin Books, 1978.
Jones, A. H. M: *Constantine and the Conversion of Europe*, Pelican Books, 1972.
Kedourie, Elie, (ed.): *The Jewish World – Revelation, Prophecy and History*, Thames & Hudson, 1979.
Keller, Werner: *The Bible as History*, Hodder & Stoughton, 1980.
Lewis, Bernard: *What Went Wrong? – The Clash between Islam and Modernity in the Middle East*, Weidenfeld & Nicolson, 2002.
Maccoby, Hyam: *Revolution in Judaea* – Jesus and the Jewish Resistance, Orbach & Chambers, 1973.
— *The Mythmaker: Paul and the Invention of Christianity*, Weidenfeld & Nicolson, 1986.
Mawdudi, Sayyid Abul A'la: *Towards Understanding the Qur'an*, Vols. 1 and 2, translated and edited by Zafar Ishaq Ansari, The Islamic Foundation, Leicester, UK, 1989.
Moore, George Foot: *Judaism in the First Centuries of the Christian Era*, Vol. 2, Cambridge, Mass., 1958.
Nietzsche, Friedrich: *The Anti-Christ*, Penguin Classics, 1968.
Parkes, James: *The Foundations of Judaism and Christianity*, 1960.
Plutarch: *Moralia*, Volume 5, The Loeb Classical Library.
— *Parallel Lives*, Volume 1, The Loeb Classical Library.
Price, Richard: *Augustine*, Fount Paperbacks, HarperCollins, 1996.
Revised Standard Version of *The Holy Bible*. Revised edition of 1946–1952, Collins, London, 1971.
Runes, Dagobert: *The War Against the Jew*, New York, Philosophical Library, 1968.
Ruthven, Malise: *A Fury for God – The Islamist Attack on America*. Granta Books, 2004.

Sabine, George H: *A History of Political Theory*, Harrap, 1937.

Saggs, H. W. F: *The Babylonians*, Macmillan Publishers Ltd / Folio Society, 1962, 1988.

Sanders, E. P: *Paul and Palestinian Judaism*, SCM Press, 1977.

Sardar, Ziauddin and Malik, Zafar Abbas: *Introducing Islam*, Icon Books UK, 2001.

Schonfield, Hugh: *Jesus – Man, Mystic, Messiah*, Open Gate Press, 2004.

Vaux, Roland de: *Ancient Israel – Its Life and Institutions*, Darton, Longman & Todd, 1973.

Vermes, Geza: *The Dead Sea Scrolls in English*, Penguin, 1962.

— *The Changing Faces of Jesus*, Penguin, 2001.

Werfel, Franz: *Paulus unter den Juden* [Paul Among the Jews], Zsolnay, 1926.

Winter, Paul: *On the Trial of Jesus*, Berlin, 1961.

Wintle, Justin: The Rough Guide *History of Islam*, 2003.

Index

S

Sabbath 53, 99
Sacrifice 14, 15, 16, 53, 55, 57, 84, 85, 102, 104, 105
— human sacrifice 26, 27, 84
Sadducees 50, 54, 55, 56, 66, 96, 97
Sadism 73, 85
Saggs, H. W. F. 60 (2)
Salvation 87, 88, 89, 93, 94, 100, 106, 109, 162
Samuel 34, 35
Sanders, E. P. 65, 75, 122 (4)
Sasanian empire 137, 138, 139, 153
Satan 76, 99, 108, 109, 118
Saudi Arabia 128
Saul (see Paul of Tarsus)
Saul, King of Israel 35
Schonfield, Hugh 65
Scribes 48, 49
Scripture 56
Seleucids 52
Self 144, 161
— self-image 4, 10
Septuagint 95
Sermon on the Mount 80
Seth 17
Sexuality 11, 12, 25, 26, 104, 106, 119, 132, 164, 165
— sexual pleasure 132-133
— sexual repression 11-12
Shamans 140
Shemaiah 55
Sicily 71
Sinai 5, 6, 23, 29
Sin 13, 14, 37, 38, 39, 41, 92, 99, 101, 105, 106, 108, 110, 114, 120, 132, 133, 149, 162
— Original sin 104, 110, 113, 161
Slaves 31, 35, 44, 60 (6), 92, 151
Society 111, 121
— authoritarian society 45
— classless society 36
Sodom and Gomorrah 28

Solomon, King of Israel 38, 39, 93
Soul 3, 8, 13, 17, 104
Spain 157, 159
— Kingdoms of Leon and Castile 159
Spirit 17, 86, 104, 106, 163
— universal Spirit 53
Splitting process 100, 163
Stalin, Josef 36
Stephen, protomartyr 94, 103
Structuralism 60 (13)
Submission 15, 146, 159, 160, 161, 163
Sudais, Sheikh Abd al-Rahman al- 127, 128
Sumeria 18
Superego 9, 11, 27, 36, 37, 50, 70, 103, 105, 110, 144, 170
Symbol(ism) 60, 71, 73, 75
Symbolisation 35
Symbolon 72
Synagogue 36, 42, 48, 94, 98
Syria 20, 39, 51, 52, 71, 141, 143, 153, 156

T

Taboo 12, 84
Talmud 36, 50
Tephillin 28
Terah 20, 22, 23
Thanatos 56
Theology 54, 119, 161
Time and Space 7, 147
Titans 73
Torah 6, 30, 35, 36, 42, 48, 49, 50, 54, 55, 56, 81, 90, 148
Totem 85
Trauma 133, 144
Tree of Knowledge 11, 84
Tree of Life 12, 84, 102
Tree of Martyrdom 102
Tribalism 53, 69, 138
Trinity 119
Truth 54, 156, 167
Tyrants 35, 36